LITTLE BOOK OF
ASTON VILLA

LITTLE BOOK OF

ASTON VILLA

First published in the UK in 2007

© G2 Entertainment Limited 2014

www.G2ent.co.uk

Printed and bound in Europe

ISBN 978-1-782812-61-6

Contents

Agbonlahor

GABRIEL AGBONLAHOR HAS GIVEN his footballing life to Villa and is now the club's highest-goalscorer in the Premier League, beating the previous total of Dwight Yorke.

He joined Villa as a boy and made his way through the ranks, making a name for himself as a prolific scorer - including 40 in one season for the youth team - before being handed his debut by David O'Leary in March 2006.

Villa were struggling at the time and were on the receiving end of a 4-1 drubbing by Everton, although Agbonlahor scored a stunning goal on his debut. He made two more starting appearances that season before really making his presence felt during Martin O'Neill's first campaign in charge.

While under O'Neill he was a regular in the side and chipped in with his fair share of goals while his blistering pace also set up chances for team-mates. His form was recognised by England in 2008 when he earned three caps over the next 12 months but failed to score in any of his appearances.

A firm favourite with the Villa fans he has now played nearly 300 games for the club, scoring more than 60 goals, and is seen as one of the team's leaders having already captained the side of several key occasions.

RIGHT Gabriel Agbonlahor during a match against Middlesbrough in April 2007

OPPOSITE Charlie Aitken later ran an antiques shop after he retired

Aitken

CHARLIE AITKEN HOLDS THE record for the most League appearances for Aston Villa. The left-back appeared in 561 League games for the club between August 1959 and May 1976 – over a staggering 17 seasons – and played in 660 games overall. The Scot was born in Edinburgh on 1 May 1942 and began his career with Gorsebridge Juniors and Edinburgh Thistle before his talents took him to Aston Villa. Over 17 years, Aitken progressed through the reserves and made his first team debut against Sheffield Wednesday in 1961 where his staunch performance as left-back saw him cement his position as a vital part of the defence.

Aitken was part of the Third Division championship winning side in 1972 and had previously won two League Cup runners-up medals (1963 and 1971) before being on the winning side in 1975 (that same year he was voted "Midland Footballer of the Year"). With his dedication and loyalty to the club, Aitken was a successful captain for the first team and his final League match for Villa was against Sheffield

ABOVE Charlie Aitken (middle row, second from the right) with the Aston Villa team, 1969

Wednesday, just as his first had been. He left Villa Park for the other side of the Atlantic where he joined New York Cosmos to play alongside the legendary Pelé. Aitken had been capped once by Scotland in 1961-62 and won two caps in the Under-23 team the following season.

Angel

WITH A FEE OF £9.5 MILLION, JUAN Pablo Angel became Aston Villa's record signing in January 2001. After six years at the club, it was announced in April 2007 that the Colombian footballer would be playing Major League Soccer in the US when he transferred to Red Bull New York. The striker began his illustrious career with Atlético Nacional in Medellín, Colombia before he was sold to River Plate in Argentina.

When he signed for Aston Villa, Angel took some time to settle in at Villa Park, but the shaky start wasn't enough to dampen the enthusiastic fans and convinced Doug Ellis that he had done the right thing in paying such an enormous fee for the young player. Angel scored 16 goals in the Premiership and became the club's top scorer during the 2003-04 season. He became a favourite with the fans, however, he lost some of his magnetic form during the following season when he only managed to find the back of the net on seven occasions.

During his time with the club, Ángel managed 62 goals in 205 games across all competitions. Only two play- ers have scored more goals for Villa in the Premier League; Dwight Yorke with 97 goals in 288 games and Gabby Agbonlahor with more than 70 goals and still going strong.

ABOVE Juan Pablo Angel competes for the ball with Pascal Chimbonda of Tottenham Hotspur

Atkinson

TAKING OVER FROM JOZEF VEGLOS, 'Big Ron' led Aston Villa to second place in the inaugural Premier League season in 1992-93 and to victory in the League Cup in 1994, securing (ultimately short-lived) UEFA Cup campaigns for both of these successes.

As of 2014, Atkinson's second place remains the highest ever finish by an English manager in the Premier League, subsequently matched only by Kevin Keegan in 1995-96.

Despite leading Villa to their first major success since their 1982 European Cup triumph, a mutual disliking between Villa chairman Doug Ellis and Ron that developed from 1992, inevitably resulted in him being sacked on 10 November 1994

following a 4–3 defeat at the hands of Wimbledon – three days after Ellis had given Ron a 'vote of confidence' in the media, stating that Atkinson was one of England's top three football managers.

By this stage, an ageing Villa side that had so nearly won the league title 18 months earlier were now among the relegation battlers. He was replaced by club legend Brian Little who kept Villa in the top flight and built a new younger team.

Atkinson began his managerial career more than 40 years ago when he retired from playing for Oxford United, his one and only club where he still holds the record for the most appearances. His first post was with non-League Kettering Town where success led him to League team Cambridge United. However, Atkinson's big break came in 1978 when he managed First Division West

Bromwich Albion.

Interestingly, Atkinson, who had been accused of racist comments during his career, was the manager who first signed three black players for his new club in Brendon Batson, Laurie Cunningham and Cyrille Regis. The three players did more than any other League players at the time to dispel racism in English football and began the trend for players of ethnic minorities to prove that they rated just as highly as their contemporaries.

It was Atkinson's continued success that saw him take up the managerial position at Manchester United in June 1981. The club did well under his leadership and during his first season finished in third place in the First Division. The club made two appearances at Wembley in the following season (1982- 83) and again finished third in the League. The following two campaigns were not as successful and the side finished fourth in the First Division both times. Further dips in form saw Atkinson sacked in 1986.

He returned to West Brom, and also had spells at Atlético Madrid, Sheffield Wednesday before joining Villa. His nomadic managerial career continued at Coventry (1995-96), again at Wednesday (1997-98) and Nottingham Forest (1999)

before he continued his already established career as a television pundit until his controversial racist comments curtailed his broadcasting work.

He still can be occasionally seen and heard as a football pundit where his idiosyncratic turns of phrase has led to his utterances becoming known as "Big-Ronisms" or "Ronglish".

BELOW Ron Atkinson, 1995

Attendances

WHILE DOUG ELLIS INSISTED ON improving the team's performance by spending any spare money on new play-ers during his tenure as chairman, present owner Randy Lerner has made it clear that increasing the number of seats is one of his main priorities.

Indeed the club's two best attendances in the Premier League (both against Liverpool - 45, 347 on May 7 1994; and 42,788 on December 29 200) are meager in comparison to the likes of Manchester United and Arsenal, and show just how vital it is for club to be able to house more fans and increase its revenues and buying power.

Of course, the ground's biggest ever crowd is a lot higher; a massive 76,588 packed into the stadium for the FA Cup 6th round tie against Derby County on 2 March 1946. They were treated to a thrilling encounter but went home deflated after Villa lost 3-4 to the eventual winners of that season's competition.

Those heady days have long gone and since the introduction of all-seater stadia which replaced the traditional terraces in the 1990s following the Hillsborough disaster, attendances have not reached anywhere near that figure. Indeed, average crowds at Villa fall a long way short of the 40,000 mark but will of course increase if the team finds success on the pitch.

Baros

MILAN BAROS MADE A £6.5 MILLION move to Villa Park in August 2005 following a successful four-year career at Liverpool. The Czech Republic player was impressive at Euro 2004 in Portugal and was the tournament's top scorer with five goals. The striker was born in Valasske Mezirici on 28 October 1981 and began his career with Banik Ostrava before signing for Liverpool in December 2001.

Gérard Houllier was keen to sign the exceptional striker having seen Baros perform in the Under-21 European Championship in 2001. During his 14 Under-21 appearances, Baros scored nine goals and displayed exceptional control. His first full cap set him on the road to stardom when he scored against Belgium. He was renowned for his constant goalscoring abilities and quickly became a regular for his national side.

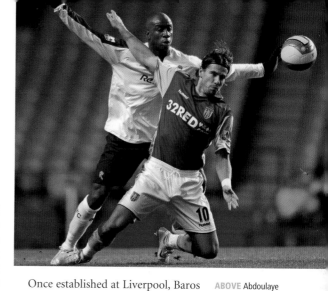

Once established at Liverpool, Baros found the back of the net no less than 12 times during the 2002-03 campaign. The following season saw him further his form until a tackle with Markus Babbel (on loan from Liverpool to Blackburn Rovers), left him with a broken ankle. His injury left him on the bench for much of the rest of the season – internationally however, he was flying high with 11 goals. A lack of action for Baros at Liverpool saw him sign for Aston Villa where, in 29 appearances, he netted 12 times. Following a difficult season under Martin O'Neill, Baros signed for Lyon, the French champions, in January 2007.

ABOVE Abdoulaye Faye of Bolton battles for the ball with Milan Baros, 2006

RIGHT Barry in action
for England against
Estonia

Barry

IF GARETH BARRY HAD BEEN blessed with just a tad more pace, he would no doubt have been heralded as one of the great British mid-fielders of this generation. As it is, he has had a fine career with more than a half-century of England caps and nearly 700 appearances for the very top Premier League teams.

Born on 23 February 1981 in Hastings, East Sussex, Barry began his illustrious Villa career in 1997 having been signed from Brighton and Hove Albion as a trainee and started as a central defender where he made up the back three with Ugo Ehiogu and Gareth Southgate.

He soon found his feet in midfield and over the course of the next decade became club captain and was one of the team's most influential and important players. He left, somewhat acrimoniously, for Man City in June 2009 for a fee of £15 million saying he wanted to play in the Champions League.

He is now out on loan at Everton but his Villa record – 441 appearances, with 52 goals – ensures that he remains a legend at the club.

Barton

THE TALENTS OF ASTON VILLA manager Tony Barton were evident for all to see during the season of 1981-82 when the club won the European Cup final just months after he took charge. Anthony Edward Barton was born on 8 April 1936 in Sutton, Surrey and took over as manager of Villa in February 1982. He remained a loyal and dedicated employee of the club until May 1984.

Barton's love of football began at an early age and he won five Youth caps and a Schoolboy cap before his career began as a trainee for Fulham. He was loaned to Sutton United before turning professional for Fulham in May 1954. Playing on the outside-right, Barton netted eight goals in 49 appearances for the club before signing for Nottingham Forest in December 1959. He never found his feet with the club, however, and scored only once in his 22 appearances for Forest and moved to Portsmouth just two years later. It was here that Barton became a player-coach and after 130 appearances and 34 goals, he hung up his boots and retired as a player. However, he came into his own on the coaching staff.

He joined the coaching team at Aston Villa and in 1980 became assistant manager to Ron Saunders. Villa claimed the League title the following year – the first time they had done so in 71 years. When Saunders unexpectedly resigned in February 1982, the obvious choice to replace him was Barton. He followed the club's success with victory over Bayern Munich in the European Cup in 1982 and the following year took his team to further victory in the European Super Cup. However, League performances were not as impressive and chairman Douglas Ellis – "who would not tolerate anything but success" – sacked Barton in May 1984.

He was replaced by Graham Turner two months later, who like Barton, managed to hold on to his position for two years. In the same month that Turner succeeded Barton, the former Villa manager took over at Northampton Town. The following year, Barton suffered a heart attack and his days with his new club were over. He became assistant manager at Southampton working with Chris Nicholl then became assistant manager at Portsmouth before the sacking of Frank Burrows saw him take the hotseat in February 1991. After much ill health, Tony Barton died of a heart attack on 20 August 1993.

ABOVE On leaving Portsmouth in 1991, Tony Barton became a talent scout for several clubs

Benteke

CHRISTIAN BENTEKE QUICKLY became a popular player with the Villa faithful since joining in the summer of 2012. In his first two seasons with the club, the burly centre forward notched a goal every other game in his 60-odd appearances.

He led the line superbly and gave Villa a real presence up top after joining the club from Genk, where he had scored 19 goals in just 37 appearances during the 2011-12 season.

Benteke's international career began at a young age for Belgium, appearing 24 times at youth level before making his senior debut in May 2010 against Bulgaria, after being picked for the squad by his former coach at Kortrijk, Georges Leekens.

He is now a regular in the squad but tragically a freak training ground injury at Villa in April when he ruptured his achilles meant that he played no part in the 2014 World Cup in Brazil.

Bodymoor Heath

ASTON VILLA'S TRAINING GROUND at Bodymoor Heath has recently undergone a major redevelopment with the first phase completed in the summer of 2007. The land – situated near the M42 – was bought from a local farmer by Doug Ellis in the early 1970s and the complex was considered state of the art when it first opened. Many players have homes in the area so they can be close to the ground, located in a rural and desirable part of Warwickshire.

Villa have been trying to modernise the facilities for many years but were repeatedly hindered by planning restrictions until plans were announced in November 2005 to update Bodymoor Heath. The facility was overhauled at an estimated cost of £8 million and now boasts four pitches, new changing rooms and a health and fitness suite to rival any in the world. The latter includes a swimming pool, underwater treadmills as well as hot and cold therapy pools all designed to keep the players fit and speed up their return from any injury suffered. The second phase of the development comprised the construction of dining and conference rooms together with offices.

ABOVE Icy conditions force the Aston Villa players to warm up in a heated tent, 2007

OPPOSITE Peter Withe (left), manager Tony Barton and goalkeeper Nigel Spinks (right) with the European Cup. They beat Bayern Munich 1-0 in the final

Bosnich

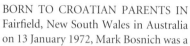

BOSNICH

BELOW Mark Bosnich takes the ball cleanly against Liverpool, 1997

BORN TO CROATIAN PARENTS IN Fairfield, New South Wales in Australia on 13 January 1972, Mark Bosnich was a star goalkeeper who became renowned for being one of the best Australian players in history. Despite his reputation as an international goalkeeper, it was Bosnich's time at Aston Villa that firmly established his career while his spells at Manchester United and Chelsea also helped to raise his profile.

It was during the League Cup semi-final in 1994 against Tranmere Rovers that Bosnich is best remembered. It was his exceptional skills that saw the Australian make three stunning penalty saves as Aston Villa beat their opponents in the penalty shootout. It set Bosnich on the road to international glory where he went on to make 22 appearances for his country – even scoring a

goal with a late penalty in a 13-0 victory over the Solomon Islands.

It all began for the goalkeeper when he started playing for local team Sydney Croatia in the Australian National Soccer League. Aged just 16, Bosnich travelled to the UK to play initially for Manchester United's youth team on a three-year contract but after only three appearances for the club, Bosnich was denied a work permit and was forced to return to his native Australia. However, his ties to the UK were made permanent when he married a UK resident and he was able to return having been lured by

Aston Villa's then boss Ron Atkinson.

After Bosnich's success in that League Cup semi-final, Villa went on to win the final against Manchester United and Bosnich further impressed his club when he played a vital role in the 1996 League Cup which once again saw Villa claim the trophy. After a total of 227 appearances for Villa, the Australian moved back to Old Trafford in 1999 where he succeeded Peter Schmeichel as the first team goalkeeper. He didn't fare well under Sir Alex Ferguson and moved to Chelsea on a free transfer in 2001.

But life was to spiral downwards for Bosnich and following a bitter marriage break-up he then tested positive for drugs in 2002. In December that year he was charged by the FA for bringing the game into disrepute and was given a nine-month ban. Following a disciplinary hearing that was initially postponed, Bosnich brought a case of unfair dismissal against Chelsea. The FA found in favour of the club and Bosnich was left with depression and no job. He is now smiling again as a media pundit (based in Australia) offering frequent fascinating observations on Talksport radio.

Bremner

DESMOND GEORGE BREMNER was born on 7 September 1952 in Aberchirder, Banffshire, in Scotland. As a midfielder, his most memorable time with Aston Villa was as part of the European Cup winning team in 1982. His career began more than 10 years earlier with Deveronvale before the Scotsman moved to Hibernian in 1971.

RIGHT Des Bremner, pictured in 1983, became the oldest player to appear for Walsall at 37 years and 240 days in May 1990

BELOW Des Bremner during a match at Villa Park, 1981

He signed for Aston Villa in 1979 for a fee of £275,000 and quickly earned himself a regular first team place. He was an instrumental part of the squad when, during Bremner's second season with the club, Villa took the League title – the first time the side had done so in 71 years. He moved to Birmingham City in October 1984 and helped his new side back into the Second Division. He went on to play for Fulham five years later but joined Walsall in 1990 and retired as a player in 1991 following a short spell with Stafford Rangers.

His career then took him to the Professional Footballers' Association where he became a director of the finance department. Bremner won one cap for Scotland in 1976 in a game against Switzerland where he replaced Kenny Dalglish on the field. His 174 appearances for Villa saw Bremner score nine goals.

Centenary

HAVING PLAYED THEIR DEBUT match in March 1874, Aston Villa celebrated their centenary season in 1973-74. Expectations at Villa Park were high following the club's third place finish in the Second Division the previous campaign when they had missed out on an automatic return to the top flight by 11 points.

The club had just spent two seasons in the Third Division – the only time in their history that they had slipped so low in the League – but had claimed the 1971-72 title with 19 goals from striker Andy Lochhead. The Bald Eagle had been signed from Leicester City in February 1970 for £30,000 but was sold to Oldham Athletic for £15,000 at the start of the centenary campaign and it was a lack of goals that saw Villa finish in the bottom half of the table.

The season had kicked off in buoy-ant mood with a 2-0 home victory over Preston North End courtesy of goals from Charlie Aitken and Trevor Hockey and Villa would remain undefeated until the end of September. Unfortunately, five of the first seven games ended in a draw (the only other victory coming against Oxford United). A 5-0 thrashing of Cardiff City on 6 October gave the Villa Park faithful hope that their stars had found their scoring form but a barren spell between November and January saw the team score just one goal in seven League games away from home.

The misery was compounded when star midfielder Bruce Rioch was sold to

ABOVE Jim Cumbes, goalkeeper for Aston Villa, March 1973

OPPOSITE Tottenham Hotspur's Paul Miller slides in on Tony Morley during the FA Charity Shield match, 1981

BELOW The FA Cup final between Aston Villa and Everton at Crystal Palace

Derby County for £200,000 in February (he went on to inspire the Rams to the First Division title the following season). The Villans enjoyed a four-game winning streak in March and April that helped to alleviate any relegation worries but the campaign finished with just one victory in the last eight matches – a 3-1 victory at home to Nottingham Forest.

Ray Graydon scored one of Villa's goals in that game and he would finish the club's joint top scorer – with Brian Little – in the League with eight goals. The pair would hit a rich vein of form the following season, netting 19 and 20 times respectively as Villa claimed the runners-up spot behind Manchester United and a return to the top flight.

The knockout competitions provided little cheer during 1973-74 either, with Villa losing their second round encounter against York City in the League Cup and Burnley ending their FA Cup dreams in the fifth round.

Charity/ Community Shield

THE FA CHARITY SHIELD EVOLVED from the Sheriff of London Shield that saw a professional club take on an amateur outfit. In 1908, this was changed to a match involving the First Division champions (Manchester United) and the Southern League champions (Queens Park Rangers) in a game that was replayed for the only time in the Shield's history. The criteria for the two sides involved in the match changed over the years until it was decided the Shield should be contested by the First Division champions and the FA Cup winners in 1930. This has remained the case to date with a few exceptions such as when the same team wins both the trophies.

Ironically, Aston Villa's invitation to play in the 1972 Charity Shield was because they were Third Division champions and their opponents were Manchester City, who had finished fourth in the First Division. A penalty from City's Francis Lee provided the

only goal of the game as Villa lost their fifth Charity Shield match.

Their third appearance – having lost to and beaten Corinthians in 1900 and 1901 – had been in 1910 when, as Division One champions, they were invited to play against Brighton & Hove Albion who had topped the Southern League. The Sussex outfit claimed the

BELOW Peter Withe on the attack, during the FA Charity Shield match against Tottenham Hotspur, 1981

trophy with the only goal of the game at Stamford Bridge.

Aston Villa next qualified for the Charity Shield by winning the 1957 FA Cup. Two goals from Peter McParland countered one from Tommy Taylor and earned his side a 2-1 victory over the Busby Babes in what has proved to be Villa's last FA Cup triumph to date. Having denied United the Double, the Old Trafford outfit gained their revenge with a 4-0 thumping of the Midlanders in the Charity Shield. Taylor scored a hat-trick while Johnny Berry completed the rout.

The closest Aston Villa have come to again winning the trophy was in 1981 when they drew 2-2 with Tottenham Hotspur. Villa were on a high and had claimed the League title the previous season and would finish the 1981-82 campaign with the European Cup in their trophy cabinet. Unfortunately two goals from Peter Withe were not enough to see off the FA Cup holders at Wembley and the trophy was shared. Withe was joint top scorer in the First Division with 20 goals, but while Spurs striker Steve Archibald also registered the same number of goals that season, it was Mark Falco who scored a brace in the Charity Shield.

Cowans

AS A CURRENT YOUTH TEAM coach, Gordon "Sid" Cowans is more than familiar with Aston Villa – the club that he joined on three separate occasions as a player himself. Born in Durham on 27 October 1958, Cowans first joined Villa as an apprentice in 1974 when he was just 15 years old and was an integral part of the side that went on to win the FA Youth Cup which saw Cowans receive his first team call-up in 1975.

The 1976-77 season saw the young player establish himself as a regular in a Villa side that won the League Cup. The midfielder was renowned for his exceptional control and his skills on the pitch earned him the 1979-80 PFA Young Player of the Year. Cowans was stoic in midfield as Villa went on to win the League in 1980-81 and was a pivotal part of the side which was to see Villa gain victory in the European Cup against Bayern Munich a year later. The following season, Cowans and Villa reached the semi-finals trying to defend their European title but were disappointed when Juventus knocked them out of the tournament. There was some consolation, however, when Cowans scored a penalty in the victory over Barcelona that brought the European Super Cup to Villa Park.

By this time, the young midfielder had

BELOW Cowans was valued at £400,000 in the deal that took him and Paul Rideout to Bari

attracted the attention of England boss Bobby Robson who gave Cowans his first full cap. But, tragedy struck when he broke his leg in a friendly against Spain which saw the midfielder out of action for the 1983-84 season. When Graham Taylor took the helm at Villa, Cowans was sold in 1985 to Italian side Bari. Villa fans were devastated by the loss of "Sid" as he was nicknamed.

In his second season for the Italian club, under new manager Enrico Catuzzi, Cowans was more on the pitch than off as Catuzzi struggled to find a winning formula for his new club. After two years abroad, Cowans made it known he wanted to return to English football and Graham Taylor quickly brought the midfielder home. Taylor was then appointed England manager and he picked Cowans to face the Republic of Ireland in a Euro 1992 qualifying match. He moved to Blackburn Rovers for two years before his third spell at Villa in 1993. He stayed for a year and made 11 appearances for the club. Before he retired as a player in 1997, Cowans played for Wolves, Sheffield United and Stockport County. He won 10 caps for England and found the back of the net on two occasions.

Delaney

WELSH DEFENDER MARK DELANEY began his career with Carmarthen in the League of Wales before coming to the attention of Cardiff manager Frank Burrows. Born in Haverfordwest on 13 May 1976, Delaney joined Cardiff on a free transfer on 1 June 1998 and made 35 appearances. Less than a year later, Delaney found himself on the way to Aston Villa in a transfer deal that cost the club £250,000 in March 1999.

The right-back made a good impression at his new club although he spent much of his early days playing for the reserves. Despite repetitive knee injuries, Delaney continued to impress at Villa and made 39 appearances in the 2001-02 season where his place in the first team became firmly established. The result was a four-year contract for the young player who was also proving himself in the Welsh national side – especially

in their famous victory over Germany. (Delaney made 36 appearances for Wales.) But injury hindered his opportunities in 2002-03 after Delaney broke his foot and the following season wasn't much better as further injuries saw him remain on the bench. In the end, his knee problem proved so persistent that Delaney retired after more than 150 League games for Villa at the age of 31 in 2007 and he returned to Villa a couple of years later as youth team coach.

ABOVE Mark Delaney lunges to tackle Arsenal's Marc Overmars, 1999

Derbies

IT IS NOT SURPRISING FOR A CITY the size of Birmingham to have two top class football clubs that were both formed many years ago when professional football was in its fledgling years. As the UK's second city, Birmingham boasts Aston Villa – formed in 1874 – and Birmingham City, established the following year as Small Heath. History books record their first clash as being played at Small Heath's Muntz Street ground on 27 September 1879. The home side won this match by one disputed goal.

With Villa being founder members of the Football League in 1888, it wasn't until Small Heath joined the newly formed Second Division in 1892 that there was any chance of the two teams meeting in a competitive fixture. Small Heath gained promotion to the top flight two years later and the intense rivalry between the two clubs began with a 1 September clash at Villa Park to open the 1894-95 season. The home side won this encounter 2-1 with goals from Steve Smith and Robert Gordon but drew the return in October 2-2. Gordon, a

Scottish striker, was signed from Hearts in May 1894 but found himself moving

The two clubs have been paired once in the FA Cup and that was in the third round of the 1900-01 competition. A goal-less draw at Muntz Street was followed by a single goal victory at Villa Park courtesy of centre-forward William Garraty. The Villans unfortunately lost against Sheffield United in the semi-final of that season's competition.

The League Cup has been a different story with the first meeting of the two clubs in the 1962-63 Final. The blue half of Birmingham emerged victorious from this encounter, winning the home leg 3-1 before a goal-less draw at Villa Park. The sides clashed again in the second round of the 1988-89 competition. This time Villa got their revenge with a comprehensive 7-0 thrashing of their neighbours over the two-legged tie. Aston Villa again met Birmingham City in the second round five years later with a similar outcome. A 1-0 scoreline in each leg gave the Villa Park outfit the opportunity to progress.

The two clubs have also faced each other in the Simod Cup, Villa winning the fixture by an emphatic 6-0 margin with goals from Alan McInally (2), David Platt, Bernard Gallacher, Derek Mountfield and Alan Evans.

on to Leicester Fosse just five months later after making four appearances.

Double

ASTON VILLA WERE CERTAINLY the team to beat in the first full decade of the Football League's existence. They had won the First Division title in 1893-94 and 1895-96 but the following season went one better by claiming the FA Cup and becoming only the second team to win the Double. This feat would remain unequalled until Tottenham Hotspur's triumphant 1960-61 campaign.

Preston North End were the first team to achieve the Double, and this occurred in the League's inaugural season. They only played 22 League games but remained undefeated – the only other team to have since managed this was Arsenal in 2003-04 – with the only points they dropped coming in a 1-1 home draw with Villa and away draws with Accrington, Blackburn and Burnley. Indeed, the Villa Park outfit finished the campaign as runners-up but were 11 points behind the champions.

Villa had signed two players who would prove to be influential in the 1896-97 season: goalkeeper Jimmy Whitehouse and winger Fred Wheldon. "Diamond" Wheldon, signed from neighbouring Small Heath, would finish as the club's top scorer with 18 League and four FA Cup goals to his name.

Although Villa registered a 2-1 win over Stoke City on the opening day of the season, they lost two and drew two of the first six games and were languishing in mid-table. Their six-point tally, however, was exactly the same as they had earned at the same stage of the previous season. A winning streak of four consecutive victories soon put the title

challenge back on track and Villa only dropped points in a further five games, losing against Burnley and Sunderland while drawing with Bury and Liverpool (twice). They finished their campaign on 47 points, 11 ahead of second placed Sheffield United, to claim their third title in four seasons.

Villa's FA Cup trail started with a 5-0 thrashing of Second Division Newcastle United and they disposed of Notts County in the following round.

It took the Villans three attempts to overcome Preston North End in the third round, with 1-1 and 0-0 draws preceding a 3-2 victory in a second replay that was staged at Bramall Lane. Liverpool were summarily dispatched 3-0 in the semi-final to set up a meeting with fellow Merseysiders Everton. The final at Crystal Palace was a hard fought affair with the Midlanders emerging 3-2 victors with goals from John Campbell, Fred Wheldon and Jimmy Crabtree.

ABOVE The victorious Aston Villa team: (back row, l-r) Secretary George Ramsay, unknown, Howard Spencer, Jimmy Whitehouse, Albert Evans, Jimmy Crabtree (front row, l-r) Jimmy Cowan, Charlie Athersmith, Johnny Campbell, John Devey, Fred Wheldon, John Cowan, John Reynolds

Dublin

FORWARD DION DUBLIN WAS born in Leicester on 22 April 1969 and arrived at Villa Park in November 1998. His career got off to a good start when he found the back of the net twice on his debut and then scored a hat-trick on his second appearance for the club. His magnetic partnership with Julian Joachim seemed the perfect ingredient for the club.

His football days began as a school-boy when he played for Wigston Fields in Leicester before signing professional terms for Norwich City in 1985 when he left school. He left three years later having never made the first team and moved to Cambridge United where his exceptional goalscoring saw the Fourth Division team climb the ranks to the Second Division, reaching the sixth round of the FA Cup in 1990-91.

At the end of the 1991-92 season, Dublin was signed for £1 million by Alex Ferguson for Manchester United but plans were scuppered when Dublin broke his leg and missed the 1992-93 campaign. The following season saw his fitness return but Eric Cantona often beat Dublin to a first team place and after a brief flirtation with the idea of moving to Everton he remained at United until he was sold to Coventry City for £2 million.

For the next four years, Dublin proved himself as one of the Premiership's leading goalscorers and it was Villa that snapped him up for £4.5 million when he became available in 1998. His seven goals in his first three games for his new club stood Dublin in good stead but fate was to hand him an unfair "card" when he seriously broke his neck in 1999 in a game against Sheffield Wednesday. As a result, Dublin now has a permanent titanium plate in his neck, holding three vertebrae together.

April 2000 saw Dublin back on form and he helped Villa to their first FA Cup final in 43 years. The Villans lost 1-0 to Chelsea, but there was no holding back Dublin until he was loaned to Millwall in 2002 following the arrival of strikers Angel and Peter Crouch at Villa. He later returned to Villa but was given a free transfer in 2004 which saw him headed for Leicester City. In his later career, Dublin reverted to playing in defence and he signed for Celtic in 2006. It was announced in September 2006 that Dublin would return to Norwich City to play out a career that totaled more than 600 League games. Dublin took his final bow in May 2008 and went on make a name for himself as a media pundit, as well as an accomplished amateur percussionist.

LEFT Dion Dublin walks away with a souvenir after scoring a hat-trick against Southampton, 1998

Ehiogu

BORN ON 3 NOVEMBER 1972 IN London, Ugochukwu "Ugo" Ehiogu found himself in the football news in January 2007 when it was announced that the former Middlesbrough and Aston Villa defender would be joining Glasgow Rangers. The centre-back signed a one-year deal with Rangers that same month and, after all the technicalities and legalities were tied-up, travelled to his new club on 25 January. Prior to this, Ehiogu had been a stoic part of the Middlesbrough defence for six years having joined from Aston Villa in November 2000.

Despite the longevity of his stay at his former club, Ehiogu's debut at Middlesbrough was cut short four minutes into play when he suffered a hamstring injury. It was an injury that was to see him on the bench for the following four months – the player has regularly suffered from injury. The start of the 2003-04 season also saw Boro miss out on the skills of the Londoner when he endured knee problems. But following a return to fitness and form he quickly became the mainstay of Middlesbrough's defence alongside Gareth Southgate. The result was a Carling Cup victory over rivals Bolton Wanderers but the high was short-lived for Ehiogu.

The following season (2004-05) saw him once again suffering from knee

injuries which meant he was unable to participate in many of Middlesbrough's important matches. Undeterred, he agreed to move to West Bromwich Albion in January 2006 but ironically was kept at Middlesbrough due to other injuries suffered by his first team colleagues. However, in November 2006, Ehiogu travelled north to Leeds United for a two-month loan where he stayed until January 2007. The defender scored a goal after moving to Rangers at the end of that month. The exceptional overhead kick against Celtic earned him the honour of Goal of the Season as voted for by Rangers' fans and his new club triumphed in a 1-0 victory.

In his 237 appearances for Aston Villa the exciting defender hit the back of the net a total of 12 times for the club and was part of the Villa team that won the League Cup on two occasions under manager Brian Little. He has also played at international level for England four times between 1996 and 2002 following his debut against China. He scored once, in a friendly against Spain in February 2001.

Ellis

THE CONTROVERSIAL chairman and major shareholder of Aston Villa was the inimitable Doug Ellis. He joined the club in 1968 and he carried out his duties as chairman before being replaced in 1975. He remained on the board before being removed in 1979 but was back in 1982 until he sold to Randy Lerner in 2006.

During Ellis's brief absence from the club (1979-82), the team enjoyed unrivalled success and were champions of both the Football League (1981) and the European Cup (1982). Ellis came in for considerable criticism when the club were relegated in 1987, but some claim that many of the players who were sold were a necessity in order to counter spiralling debts.

Born Herbert Douglas Ellis on 3 January 1924, in Chester, his early life was particularly difficult. However, despite his disadvantaged childhood, Ellis became a successful entrepreneur

RIGHT Doug Ellis announcing the appointment of Martin O'Neill as the new manager of the club, 2006

BELOW Doug at work with the Coca Cola Cup trophy on his desk, 1994

– he owned 47% of Aston Villa in 2006 – by marketing and selling Spanish package deals. By the time he was 40, his business skills had made Ellis a millionaire.

He was renowned for his ego – the Witton Lane Stand was renamed the Doug Ellis Stand in the 1990s – and was rarely challenged over his management style or decisions, while fans often accused him of not bringing in enough top players. Ellis remains life president at the club and in March 2012, he was knighted for his charity work.

European Cup

ALTHOUGH THE EUROPEAN CUP had first been competed for in 1955-56, it wasn't until Aston Villa won the First Division title in 1980-81 that they qualified for Europe's flagship club competition. The fact that they won it at the first time of asking emulated the achievement of Nottingham Forest in 1978-79.

Villa's very first European Cup tie was at home to Valur and goals from Tony Morley, Terry Donovan (2) and Peter Withe (2) ensured the perfect start to their campaign. The return leg in Iceland saw Gary Shaw net twice to send Villa through to a second round meeting

BELOW The Villa team celebrate winning the European Cup in 1982

with Dynamo Berlin. Morley was again on target, scoring a brace, as the Villans won the away leg 2-1 so it didn't matter so much that the Germans won 1-0 at Villa Park because the Midlanders went through having scored more away goals.

It would prove to be the last goal that Villa conceded en route to the trophy as goalkeeper Jimmy Rimmer was in superb form. Dynamo Kiev were dispatched 2-0 on aggregate while a solitary Morley goal in the first leg of the semi-final was enough to see off Anderlecht. That set up a clash with Bayern Munich in Rotterdam. Even the loss of Rimmer (replaced by youngster Nigel Spink making only his second appearance for the club) after nine min-

utes could not give the Germans the advantage and Withe scored the only goal of the night to send the Villa Park faithful wild.

They began their defence of the European Cup with a home tie against Besiktas. Goals from Withe, Morley and Mortimer gave the home side a 3-1 lead after the first leg and ensured that the second leg in Turkey was merely a formality (this was drawn 0-0 to set up a clash with Dinamo Bucharest). The Romanians were no obstacle for a Villa side in full flow and a brace from Shaw in Bucharest laid the perfect foundation for an entertaining return tie at Villa Park. Shaw was again on target in the second leg, this time netting a hat-trick, and Mark Walters rounded up the scoring in a 4-2 victory. Juventus were Villa's opponents in the quarter-final but the Italians proved too strong and emerged 5-2 victors over the two-legged tie.

The closest Aston Villa have come to qualifying since was when they finished as runners-up to Manchester United in 1992-93. But even though this was the inaugural season of the UEFA Champions League it was before more than one club was allowed to compete from each country.

European Super Cup

THE EUROPEAN SUPER CUP – NOW called the UEFA Super Cup – was first competed for in 1973 and pits Europe's top two sides against each other. Traditionally played as the curtain raiser for the new season, the Cup was contested by the European Cup (UEFA Champions League since 1992-93) and European Cup Winners' Cup holders. Since the abolition of the Cup Winners' Cup following the 1998-99 final, the match has featured the UEFA Cup winners.

There have, however, been occasions such as in 1974 and 1981 when the two clubs involved have been unable to agree a convenient date for the fixture to be played and the 1985 competition was cancelled in the aftermath of the Heysel tragedy when Everton should have faced Juventus.

As European Cup holders, Villa were paired with Barcelona for the two-legged tie in January 1983. The first leg in Spain saw a solitary goal from Marcos Alonso Peña in the 52nd minute give the home side a slender advantage but no-one would have been prepared for the way Villa blew their opponents out of the water in the return match. Gary Shaw scored after 80 minutes to send the tie into extra-time and goals from Gordon Cowans and Ken McNaught sealed the victory.

BELOW Aston Villa celebrate with the UEFA Super Cup (back row, l-r) Gary Williams, Colin Gibson, Peter Withe, Nigel Spink, Gary Shaw; (front row, l-r) Andy Blair, Des Bremner, Mark Walters, Ken McNaught, Gordon Cowans, Tony Morley

FA Cup

THE FA CUP IS THE LONGEST running competition in world football, having first been contested in 1871-72. Aston Villa lie joint fourth with Liverpool in the table of clubs that have won the most FA Cups, with seven to their name (only Manchester United, Arsenal and Spurs have won more finals). Villa have also been runners-up on three occasions.

Aston Villa first entered the FA Cup in 1879-80 but had to wait until the second round to kick their first ball in the competition. They were handed a bye in the first round but faced Stafford Road for a place in the third round. A 1-1 draw at Perry Barr led to a replay which Villa won 3-1. Their opponents in the next round were Oxford University but the history books do not reveal why Aston Villa failed to turn out for this fixture and the scholars were awarded a walkover.

RIGHT Aston Villa celebrate their FA Cup semi-final victory over Bolton Wanderers in 2000. Villa won 4-1 on penalties after the game finished 0-0.

FA CUP

It didn't take long, however, for Villa to get their hands on the trophy…and when they did it ensured their place in the soon to be formed Football League. Villa registered their record Cup victory in the first round of the 1886-87 competition en route to their first ever FA Cup final…another Midland derby, this time against West Bromwich Albion.

Goals from Dennis Hodgetts and Archie Hunter secured the trophy that saw the streets of Birmingham packed with fans celebrating their famous victory.

The Villans imposed their dominance on the competition, winning the trophy another four times – 1-0 against West Brom in 1895; 3-2 against Everton in 1897 (completing the Double by claiming the First Division title); 2-0 against Newcastle United in 1905; and 1-0 against Sunderland in 1913 – before the First World War broke out. They also won the first competition following the end of hostilities with a 1-0 victory over Huddersfield Town in 1920. The Villa Park faithful then had to endure another 37 years before their team lifted the trophy with a 2-1 victory preventing Manchester United from completing their own Double in 1956-57.

As previously mentioned, Aston Villa have fallen at the final hurdle on three occasions. The first of these was in 1892 when West Brom gained their revenge with a 3-0 victory at the Oval while Newcastle United also exacted retribution with a 2-0 triumph in 1924. Villa's most recent appearance in the final was in 2000 when Chelsea scored the only goal of the game.

FA Premiership

ASTON VILLA'S BEST PERFORMANCE in the Premiership came in its inaugural 1992-93 season when they finished as runners-up to Manchester United. It was hardly an auspicious start to the campaign however, as they registered 1-1 draws in their first three games (against Ipswich Town, Leeds United and Southampton) with new signing Dalian Atkinson scoring in each match.

Atkinson, no relation to manager Ron Atkinson, was signed from Real Sociedad and went on to score 11 League goals but found himself second in the club's scoring charts behind Dean Saunders who finished the season with 13. The Welshman had been transferred from Liverpool along with team-mate Ray Houghton and the pair were an immediate success at Villa Park. Indeed, Houghton's Republic of Ireland compatriot Steve Staunton made up a trio of former Anfield favourites who were now earning their living in the Midlands.

The three would have been particularly pleased with the 4-2 victory over their former club in September but other notable wins included a 5-1 thrashing of

Middlesbrough and a home victory over Manchester United while the 10-point advantage the eventual champions enjoyed by the end of the season could have been a lot less had Villa not lost

ABOVE Patrik Berger celebrates scoring the third goal during the Premiership match against Sheffield United, May 2007

ABOVE Villa celebrate their 6-0 thrashing of Derby in 2008

1994-95 campaign saw them finish just five points clear of the relegation trap door. Atkinson made way for Brian Little who revitalised the team and lifted them to a much more respectable fourth and a UEFA Cup slot. This was followed by another top five finish but Villa struggled to make an impact in the 1997-98 campaign.

Despite bringing Stan Collymore back to the Midlands, Little found himself under pressure at the start of the New Year with his side having lost 13 and drawn six out of their 27 games. This left them precariously placed and with the papers full of speculation that Little was about to be sacked he resigned. John Gregory was brought in to rescue the club's season and he did just that, with nine wins from the remaining 11 matches thrusting his side to a respectable seventh position.

Under Martin O'Neill, Villa remained a force to be reckoned with as he guided them to three successive top six finishes. They have recently flirted with relegation under the managership of Paul Lambert who puts his faith in youth although the signing of Philippe Senderos should add some experience to the Villa defence in the 2014-15 season.

their last three League matches.

Sadly, Villa could not build on this success and slumped to 10th position the following season while the

Famous Fans

THERE ARE ALWAYS HIGH PROFILE celebrities who are associated with football clubs and Aston Villa are no exception. Perhaps the biggest name who is proud to be a Villan is Prince William even though people are probably more used to seeing him in the crowd watching his beloved England play rugby. The second in line to the throne was born less than a month after Villa claimed their only European Cup to date.

Nigel Kennedy has never been shy about his love for the Villa Park outfit and has even had his Rolls Royce painted in claret and blue. The classical violinist rose to fame in the 1980s and currently has homes in Malvern and Poland.

Other notable names who support Aston Villa include: Iain Duncan Smith (the Leader of the Conservative Party from 2001 until 2003); pop stars such as Ocean Colour Scene and former Black Sabbath frontman turned TV star Ozzy Osbourne; sporting heroes such as hockey player Jane Sixsmith; and various people from the world of television like Emma B (Radio 1 DJ), Mark Williams (*The Fast Show*) and children's TV presenter Floella Benjamin.

ABOVE Ozzy Osbourne at the Grammys

ABOVE LEFT Prince William is a famous fan

LEFT Nigel Kennedy performing at the Royal Albert Hall

Full Members' Cup

THE FULL MEMBERS' CUP WAS A competition created by the Football League to fill in the void left by the absence of European football. Following the tragic events at the Heysel Stadium in Brussels on 29 May 1985 that saw 39 football fans lose their lives while trying to watch the European Cup Final between Juventus and Liverpool, British clubs were banned from entering European competition for five years (Liverpool received an extra year's punishment).

And so it was that the Full Members' Cup came into existence, although participation was optional from the teams that made up the top two flights of English football. The inaugural competition saw a thrilling climax which saw Chelsea pip Manchester City to the title by the odd goal in nine.

Aston Villa entered the following season's tournament and got off to a flying start by beating Derby County in the second round. Goals from Gary Shaw (2), Tony Daley and Alan Evans sentenced the Rams to a 4-1 defeat at Villa Park in

November 1986. Sadly, Villa were unable to break down their third round opponents and Ipswich Town progressed to the next round with a 1-0 victory.

RIGHT Gary Shaw scored a brace against Derby but only made one other appearance during the 1986-87 campaign in a season that was blighted by injury

Gray

BORN IN GLASGOW ON 30 November 1955, Andrew Mullen Gray began his football career as a striker for Dundee United. He made 62 appearances for the club and scored a successful 46 goals before moving to Aston Villa in 1975. In his three years with Villa, Gray made 113 appearances netting the ball a respectable 54 times.

It was his 29 goals during the 1977-78 campaign that earned him the PFA Young Player of the Year award as well as the PFA Players' Player of the Year. He was the first player to win both awards, a record that was only equalled in 2007 by Ronaldo. Gray was regularly capped for Scotland and played a total of 20 international matches between 1975 and 1985. He found the back of the net on seven occasions in his 10 years as an international.

Following his growing reputation at

ABOVE Andy Gray was voted both Player and Young Player of the Year in 1977

Villa, Gray moved to Wolves in 1979 where he spent the next four years making 133 appearances and scoring 38 goals. In 1983, he headed for Everton where he netted the ball 14 times in 49 appearances over two years before returning to Villa in 1985. Gray had been a member of Everton's winning

FA Cup side in 1984 and won the First Division and a European Cup Winners' Cup medal in 1985.

Once back at Villa, Gray's goalscoring ability continued but after just a year he went to Notts County on loan before permanently transferring to West Bromwich Albion in 1987. He spent a year with the club before moving back north to join Rangers (the team he supports) between 1988 and 1989. His final club was Cheltenham Town (1989-90) and when he retired Gray found his niche as a football commentator.

He became a top class football pundit on Sky Sports but was sacked from his high-profile position following some off-air sexist remarks. He subsequently joined Talksport Radio where he still airs his views on shows with co-presenter Richard Keys who was also sacked from Sky following the same alleged incident.

One interesting trivia fact about Gray is that he acted in the movie A Shot At Glory alongside Rangers' hero Ally McCoist and Hollywood legend Robert Duvall in 2000. Oscar winner Duvall plays the manager of a second-tier Scottish club that faces increasing pressure from its US-owner, played by another Hollywood great, Michael Keaton.

BELOW Andy Gray and Paul Miller (left) of Charlton Athletic jump for the ball

Hampton

JOSEPH HARRY HAMPTON, BETTER known as Harry, was born in Wellington, Shropshire, on 21 April 1885. With his nicknames of "Happy" or "The Wellington Whirlwind", the centre-forward played for Aston Villa between 1904 and 1920 and was an impressive striker who netted the ball for his club 242 times in his 367 appearances. In fact, he is Villa's record League goalscorer with 215 goals.

He moved to Villa in April 1904 from Wellington Town and was renowned for being one of the most prolific strikers in the lead up to First World War. He was strong, forceful and dedicated and his determination and endurance meant that he was feared by goalkeepers and defenders alike. He was an exceptional player who was capped for England on four occasions for whom he found the back of the net twice.

He won a League Championship medal with Villa in 1910 to go with the FA Cup winner's medal he received in 1905 (he won the FA Cup again eight years later). He fought in the First World War and regained his fitness quickly after a gas attack suffered during action. He was back playing football following military service where he continued to hammer home the ball for Birmingham. After retiring from football Hampton became a coach and died on 15 March 1963.

ABOVE Harry Hampton played four times for England between 1913-14 and scored two goals

Hendrie

MIDFIELDER LEE HENDRIE SPENT the second half of the 2006-07 season on loan to Stoke City and is the son of former Birmingham City player, Paul Hendrie. Born in Birmingham on 18 May 1977, Lee made his debut for Villa on 23 December 1995 against Queens Park Rangers when he came on as a substitute in a 1-0 defeat but was dismissed for two bookable offences.

However, his skills on the field earned him the Young Player of the Season award for 1997-98 and his excellent touch gave Hendrie a chance to shine in the England Under-21s (he won a full cap when he came on as a substitute against the Czech Republic in 1999). However, his controversial ways were back some years later and during the 2004-05 campaign he managed to receive nine yellow cards and one controversial red card.

In November 2005, in a head-butting incident on the pitch against Manchester City, Hendrie was reluctant to leave the field following the red card. He was warned about his violent behaviour and given a three-match ban by the FA Disciplinary Commission. O'Leary had succeeded Graham Taylor – who had virtually dropped Hendrie – and was more impressed by Hendrie's 10 appearances for the club in the following season.

Under Martin O'Neill, Hendrie continued to impress during the 2006-07 campaign but was loaned to Stoke City in January 2007 before a permanent move to Sheffield United the following January. After only 12 League appearances for the Blades, however, Hendrie found himself on loan with Leicester City but was unable to prevent them from being relegated to League One.

Hendrie's personal life has proved to be just as dramatic as his professional. In 2000, Hendrie stated that he would become tee-total during the football season following his three-month ban in international games for breaking the team curfew in the England Under-21s. But, in 2003, he was banned from driving for 12 months when he was stopped by police on the M40. It was discovered that Hendrie was one and a half times over the drink-drive limit.

He married his childhood sweetheart and mother of his two children in 2004 but the marriage was over in hours after it was revealed that Hendrie had been seeing another woman. The honeymoon was cancelled and Hendrie promptly moved in with his new partner.

His off field activities have had a

great and harmful influence on his career and his is a tragic story of unfulfilled potential and since leaving the Villa he has played for myriad clubs without ever achieving a fraction of what he promised.

Hitchens

GERALD "GERRY" ARCHIBALD Hitchens was born on 8 October 1934 in Rawnsley, Staffordshire and died in 1983 from a heart attack at a charity match in Wales. Despite his young age, perhaps it was a fitting end for the centre-forward who began his professional career with Kidderminster Harriers. He joined the Harriers in August 1953 but moved to Cardiff City two years later for a transfer fee of £1,500.

He scored a dramatic goal on his League debut for Cardiff and the victory against Wolves that day helped keep his side in the First Division. At Cardiff, Hitchens built up an exceptional partnership with Trevor Ford – a former hero at Villa – and was the top goalscorer in two successive campaigns finishing with a total of 40 times in his 95 appearances for the club. In 1957, his value had significantly increased and he joined Aston Villa for £22,500.

His four seasons at Villa saw the fearless striker determined in his approach and he continued his impressive run of netting the ball. For three of the campaigns, Hitchens was Villa's leading striker between 1958 and 1961. In total, his 160 appearances for the club saw the Villan find the back of the net no less than 96 times. In November 1959, he scored five of Villa's 11 goals against Charlton in an 11-1 victory, while his exceptional style of play saw him instrumental in Villa's campaign and their winning formula saw them become the top team in the Second Division.

The following year, Villa reached the League Cup final with the help of their heroic striker. He became a regular England Under-23 player before claiming his full cap for the international side in 1961. His debut came at Wembley against Mexico and Hitchens scored just two minutes into the game. It set the team up for an 8-0 victory over their opponents. It was the first of seven full caps for Hitchens who once again proved his talents two weeks after the victory of Wembley in a match in Rome where England beat their hosts 3-2. Two of the goals were from Hitchens.

His prowess on the field brought him to the attention of Internazionale who also signed fellow players Joe Baker, Jimmy Greaves and Denis Law to play in Italy. It was the start of a six-year career in Italy that saw Hitchens

play in the Italian Serie A and Serie B. Although he scored five goals for England during his seven caps, new manager Alf Ramsey overlooked the confident striker in favour of home-based players. For three further years, Hitchens remained in Italy and played for Torino, Atalanta and Cagliari before retiring to North Wales.

Internationals

MANY INTERNATIONAL STARS from numerous countries have graced the Villa Park pitch over the years. Indeed, even as far back as 1933-34 the club boasted no fewer than 14 full internationals on their books.

Villa's most capped player of all time is Steve Staunton who also holds the record for most caps for his country. The defender won 64 of his 102 Republic of Ireland caps during his two stays at Villa Park and was selected to captain his country at the 2002 World Cup in Japan and South Korea following manager Mick McCarthy's argument with Roy Keane that saw the midfielder dismissed from the squad and sent home. Staunton's last appearance for Eire was in 2002 and he was also manager of the national side in the mid-2000s.

The club's record transfer fees paid and received have also been for international stars. They paid £9.5 million in January 2001 for Juan Pablo Angel and the Colombian striker provided many priceless goals over the next six years before his free transfer to New York Major League side Red Bull in April 2007. One of the highest transfer fees that Villa has received was the £12.6 million that Manchester United shelled out for Dwight Yorke. The Trinidad and Tobago striker joined Villa in 1989 and established himself as one of the best strikers in England prior to his August 1998 move to Old Trafford. He announced his retirement from international football in March 2007, having scored 29 goals in 59 games.

Other notable players who have

worn the claret and blue over the years and been capped at international level include the club's top League goalscorer Harry Hampton who netted 215 times in 339 League games for Villa between 1904 and 1920 but was only capped four times by England. Midfielder David Platt made his name at Aston Villa but it was his performances in an England shirt – particularly at the 1990 World Cup in Italy – that earned him a £5.5 million move to Bari in July 1991.

Villa Park has seen a host of players who have carved out successful careers representing their country including Andy Townsend (Eire), Savo Milosevic (Croatia), Gareth Southgate (England), Andy Gray (Scotland) but perhaps the position that has seen the most internationals is between the posts. Villa can boast impressive goalkeepers such as Sam Hardy, Jimmy Rimmer and Nigel Spink (all England), Peter Schmeichel (Denmark), Mark Bosnich (Australia), Thomas Sorensen (Denmark), Shay Given (Eire) and Brad Guzman (US).

ABOVE Danish goalkeeper Thomas Sorensen gives instructions to his team-mates during the Euro 2004 quarter-final match against the Czech Republic

Intertoto Cup

THE INTERTOTO CUP WAS A competition organised by UEFA that gave another chance to teams who missed out on automatic qualification into the Champions League or UEFA Cup. Teams who wished to participate must have applied for the privilege but it was a worthwhile consideration as it often leads to a lucrative European run. The competition had originally been conceived as a means of allowing betting to continue through the summer but was brought under the UEFA umbrella in 1995. The format changed in 2006-07 with three rounds played instead of the usual five. The 11 winners of the third round ties were then entered into the second qualifying round of the UEFA Cup.

Aston Villa first entered the Intertoto Cup in 2000-01 and beat Marila Pribram 3-1 on aggregate before losing their second round clash against Celta Vigo 4-2 over two legs. Unperturbed, they tried again the following season and succeeded in winning a place in the UEFA Cup with victories over Slaven Beluo, Stade Rennais and FC Basel. In 2002-03, Villa triumphed over Zurich in the third round before losing to Lille in one of the three semi-finals (the winner of each final won entry into the first round of the UEFA Cup).

James

BORN ON 1 AUGUST 1979 in Welwyn Garden City, David Benjamin James signed as a trainee with Watford in 1989 where he won the FA Youth Cup. He went on to make 98 appearances for the first team before he moved to Liverpool in 1992.

The renowned goalkeeper had a run of bad luck and his conceded goals saw him dropped by manager Graeme Souness. However, Roy Evans (Souness' successor) was keen for the young player to reach his potential and James became a regular in the first team during the 1990s. Even though Liverpool went on to claim the League Cup in 1995, James had made a number of high-profile mistakes in the club's campaign to oust Manchester United off the Premiership top spot and he earned himself the nickname "Calamity

James" within the media. In 1999 he was transferred to Aston Villa when Liverpool brought in goalkeeper Brad Friedel.

James's form continued to see-saw and he moved to West Ham in 2001 where his form dramatically improved although the club was relegated in 2003. In January 2004, he made it back into Premiership football when he signed for Manchester City where he was instrumental in helping the club keep their place in the Premiership by saving two penalties at the end of the season.

Despite some success at Manchester

ABOVE David James saves a penalty during the FA Cup semi-final between Aston Villa and Bolton Wanderers at Wembley, 2000

RIGHT David James celebrates, 1999

City, especially under the guidance of manager Stuart Pearce, James wanted to move closer to London for family reasons. He signed a deal with Portsmouth in January 2004 that allowed the goalkeeper to be nearer his children. The transfer cost new club Portsmouth £2 million, however, James did not move to the south coast until August 2006 where he signed on the dotted line for two years.

At his new club, James found the form that had often deserted him in the past and impressed boss Harry Redknapp enough to state: "...by far the best keeper I've worked with". With more than 600 League appearances to his credit, James' improved reliability and increased consistency led for calls for the former Villa goalkeeper to be reinstated to the international team. James won his first full cap in a friendly against Mexico in 1997 and was basically understudy to David Seaman, but came into his own following the stoic keeper's retirement. Now retired, with more than 800 league appearances to his credit, James bowed out on the international stage at the 2010 World Cup Finals in South Africa. Following a howler from No 1 keeper Robert Green in the opening game against the US, he was recalled to the side and played in the next three matches against Algeria, Slovenia and West Germany (where England were eliminated 4-1) and became the oldest ever World Cup debutant at the age of 39 years and 321 days.

Joachim

TEENAGE PRODIGY, JULIAN KEVIN Joachim was born in Boston, Lincolnshire on 20 September 1974. With his lightning pace and ability to confuse the opposition's defence, Joachim proved his worth in the youth team at Leicester before turning profes-

sional in September 1992. He spent four years with the club before Aston Villa signed the promising youngster in February 1996 for £1.5 million. With a regular place on the Leicester first team, the striker managed to net the ball on 31 occasions during his 119 appearances for the club.

Brian Little signed him for Villa where he found himself facing compe-

LEFT Julian Joachim is fouled by Gianluca Festa of Middlesbrough

tition from the likes of Dwight Yorke, Savo Milosevic and Tommy Johnson. He did however score on his debut for Villa against Blackburn, but the constant competition did little to improve his first team chances. It gave rise to a slow start at Villa for Joachim, however, the 1997-98 campaign proved more fruitful for the exceptional striker and a regular first team place inspired the fans and made him a firm favourite.

Like many other great players Joachim was faced with ups and downs and injuries that blighted his form. But overall, his time at Villa was spent scoring stunning goals and he was voted the club's Player of the Year in 1999. The arrival of Benito Carbone in 1999 did see Joachim on the bench on a number of occasions but a window of opportunity opened for the striker when Dion Dublin found himself out of the game for the entire season. It provided Joachim with a place on an ever skilful forward line for Villa.

It all changed for the striker in July 2001 during the summer transfer window when Joachim was sent to lower division Coventry City in a player-exchange with Mustapha Hadji which cost the club £2 million. Three years later, in June 2004, Joachim found himself heading east to Leeds United on a free transfer. The player's new club were at the time heavily in debt and in the process of trying to rebuild the team, if somewhat inexpensively. His season with Leeds was disappointing and he only managed two goals in his 27 appearances. He found himself loaned to Walsall for the final two months of the campaign. He moved to Boston United for the 2005-06 season where he joined the team in League Two. Then, on 14 August 2006, Joachim joined Darlington for £100,000 – a record fee for his new club.

BELOW Julian Joachim celebrates after scoring a goal

Kits

ASTON VILLA ARE ONE OF numerous sides in England who wear a kit comprising of claret and blue (others include West Ham United, Burnley and Scunthorpe United). But that has not always been the case; in the club's early days they wore kits that included blue/red, black and blue/white and the minutes of a meeting in November 1886 confirmed an order for two dozen chocolate/sky blue outfits.

By the 1890s, however, Villa had adopted their now famous claret and blue colours although there are several possible theories behind the reason for this decision. One suggests that the directors were unable to decide at a meeting in Birmingham's Barton's Arms and that they took their inspiration from the coloured tiles on the walls of the public house. Another, perhaps more plausible, explanation is that it was suggested by the Scottish contingent prevalent at Villa at the time and combined the blue of Glasgow Rangers with the maroon of Hearts and that the crest should include the rampant lion of Scotland.

Aston Villa ran a survey in 2006-07 to see if fans wanted to revamp the club's crest and it was announced that every fan who attended the last home game of the season would be given a free scarf bearing the new design.

ABOVE Lee Hendrie takes the ball upfield, 2000

ABOVE LEFT Paul Elliott in action against Charlton Athletic

LEFT John Carew poses with a club shirt, 2007

League Championship

BELOW Despite losing 2-0 to Arsenal in May 1981, these Villa fans are celebrating winning the League title

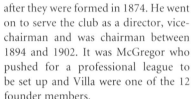

THE FORMATION OF THE FOOTBALL League in 1888 owed much to the determination of William McGregor, a Scotsman who had seen his first football match at the age of eight and who became associated with Aston Villa soon after they were formed in 1874. He went on to serve the club as a director, vice-chairman and was chairman between 1894 and 1902. It was McGregor who pushed for a professional league to be set up and Villa were one of the 12 founder members.

Aston Villa finished runners-up to Preston in the inaugural season but claimed their first title in 1893-94 with several notable performances including a 9-0 Boxing Day annihilation of Darwen. Villa dominated the 1890s in much the same way that Liverpool did in the 1970s and 1980s and Manchester United in the 1990s. They won back-to-back titles in 1895-96 and 1896-97 (the same year they triumphed in the FA Cup to claim the Double) and repeated this after finishing sixth the following season. Indeed, when they won their fifth championship in 1899-1900, they

set a new record of 50 points from 34 games. They topped the Division One table again in 1909-10 and also narrowly missed out a further five times before the advent of the First World War when they finished second.

Sadly, that was to prove their last League title for more than 70 years – although they were runners-up in 1930-31 and 1932-33 – and the unthinkable happened in 1936 when they were relegated to the Second Division for the

ABOVE Players celebrate their League Championship victory, 1981

ABOVE Captain Dennis Mortimer takes the Division One trophy on a lap of honour

first time in their history. They bounced back at the second attempt claiming the Second Division crown in 1937-38 and remained in the top flight until they suffered another relegation in 1959.

This time their stay in the second tier only lasted one season but there followed a period of instability that saw the club return to the Second Division in 1967 and drop to the Third in 1970.

Promotions in 1972 and 1975 saw Villa regain their top-flight status, a position they have held ever since apart from one season in the Second Division in 1987-88. Villa's most recent of their seven First Division titles came in 1980-81 when manager Ron Saunders used just 14 players (seven of whom were ever-present) and the club were runners-up to Liverpool in 1989-90.

League Cup

ASTON VILLA RANK SECOND ONLY to Liverpool when it comes to success in the League Cup, with eight final appearances resulting in five trophies. They have also been losing semi-finalists on five occasions since the competi- tion's debut in 1960-61.

The idea of a League Cup had been proposed as far back as 1892 yet it was only when the League Secretary Alan Hardaker pushed for its inception that it became a reality. Since then, the tournament has had several sponsors and been known as the Milk Cup (1981-86), Littlewoods Cup (1986-90), Rumbelows Cup (1990-92), Coca-Cola Cup (1992-98), Worthington Cup (1998-2003)

BELOW The team celebrate a goal during the Worthington Cup third round match against Chelsea, 1998

LEAGUE CUP

RIGHT Tony Hateley finished the 1964-65 League Cup campaign with 10 goals

Carling Cup (2003-12) until its current guise of the Capital One Cup (2012-16). Many of the bigger clubs refused to enter the competition in its early years until the final was moved to Wembley in 1967 (prior to this it had been played over two legs at the participants' home grounds) and victory ensured entry into the following season's UEFA Cup. Aston Villa were one of the top-flight teams who did enter the inaugural competition and they emerged triumphant with a 3-0 extra-time victory over Rotherham United at Old Trafford in the second leg after losing the first game at Millmoor by 2-0.

They were back in the final two years later and this time their opponents were local rivals Birmingham City but Villa lost the first leg 3-1 and could only manage a 0-0 draw in the return match. They almost made it three final appearances in five years but fell at the semi-final stage in 1965. Tony Hateley had grabbed seven goals in the earlier rounds – including four in the 7-1 fifth round demolition of Bradford City – but despite scoring another three over the two-legged clash Chelsea progressed to the final with a 4-3 aggregate score.

Villa appeared in three finals in the 1970s, claiming the trophy twice (they lost 2-0 against Spurs in 1971 but beat Norwich City 1-0 in 1975 and Everton 3-2 in 1977) but the furthest they progressed in the 1980s was two semi-finals (1984 and 1986). They did add their name to the trophy in 1994 and 1996 with victories over Manchester United (a 3-1 win against manager Ron Atkinson's former club) and Leeds United (3-0) but the closest they recently came to adding to their tally was in the 2010 Final against Manchester United where James Milner scored an early penalty, but United replied with goals from Michael Owen and Wayne Rooney.

Lerner

FANS WERE DELIGHTED WHEN American entrepreneur Randy Lerner assumed control of Villa in September 2006 after a £62.6 million takeover was agreed with the club's board.

Installing himself as chairman, the appointment was welcomed by the majority of supporters who had been trying for years to oust Doug Ellis because of his reluctance to spend enough money on new players which should have helped to bring success back to Villa Park.

In June 2011, Lerner controversially appointed manager Alex McLeish from local rivals Birmingham City , only to fire McLeish barely a year later. He replaced McLeish with then Norwich Vity manager Paul Lambert.

He invested about £20m into the club on March 2013 and waived off the £100m interest owed to him by Aston Villa due to the fact Villa were struggling financially. On May 12th, 2014, Lerner announced he had put the club up for sale, stating, "I owe it to Villa to move on, and look for fresh, invigorated leadership, if in my heart I feel I can no longer do the job."

LEFT Chairman Randy Lerner put the club up for sale in May 2014.

Little

IT ALL BEGAN FOR FORWARD BRIAN Little with Aston Villa when he signed for the then Third Division team on leaving school in 1970. Little progressed through the youth team and in his 302 appearances for the club he scored 82 times. Little, who was born on 25 November 1953 in County Durham, found himself in two League Cup winning teams for Villa in 1975 and 1977 and won a full cap for England in May 1975 against Wales at Wembley.

Despite his excellent skills on the pitch, his career was cut short when he suffered a serious knee injury in 1979. He was a favourite with the fans and had a reputation for being a Villa Park hero. But his career was far from over and Little remained on the Villa payroll as a youth team coach. He then coached the first team at Wolves who were being relegated to the Fourth Division for the first time in 1986. The debts at the club were immense and John Barnwell resigned as manager. Little took the reins on a temporary basis but was later replaced by Graham Turner.

Little then moved to Middlesbrough as first team coach but the club was also in financial difficulties and narrowly missed bankruptcy. However, with help from Little and other members of the staff, the club slowly improved and saw themselves promoted on two successive occasions to play in the First Division for the 1988-89 season. Little left for Darlington to become manager at the end of the season where his new team sat squarely at the bottom of the Football League in the Fourth Division. The end of the 1990-91 season saw his club win the Fourth Division Championship.

In June 1991, Leicester City appointed Little manager as successor to Gordon Lee and he took the Second Division club to fourth place by the end of the season. After a great deal of hard work

and determination by both manager and players, Leicester gained a place in the Premiership during the 1993-94 campaign on their third attempt.

Little earned the job of manager at Aston Villa in November 1994 and led the team to the 1996 League Cup. Four years later he was manager of Stoke City and then West Bromwich Albion in 1999. He moved to Hull City in 2000, Tranmere Rovers in 2003 and on to Wrexham in 2007. Unfortunately, the Red Dragons lost their League status with relegation from League Two at the end of 2007-08 and Little parted company to go to Northern Conference side, Gainsborough Trinity, until he was sacked in 2011.

ABOVE Aston Villa manager Brian Little celebrates, 1995

LEFT Little's knee injury was only picked up when he was undergoing a medical in anticipation of a transfer to rivals Birmingham City

OPPOSITE Brian Little is widely regarded as one of the greatest players to have played for Villa

Managers

THE VILLA PARK HOT SEAT has certainly not seen the stability enjoyed by the likes of Crewe Alexandra, Manchester United and Arsenal and has seen its fair share of managers throughout its history.

Managers such as Saunders (June 1974-February 1982) have their own entry in this book, as do Tony Barton (February 1982-May 1984), Graham Taylor (July 1987-July 1990 and February 2002-May 2003), Ron Atkinson (July 1991-November 1994), Brian Little (November 1994-February 1998), and Martin O'Neill (August 2006 – August 2010).

The club's first proper manager was Jimmy McMullan, the former Scottish international who had won the Second Division title with Manchester City in 1928. Before this, team selection had been the responsibility of the club secretary and a committee including directors and the club captain. McMullan's tenure

proved to be brief and came to an abrupt end after Villa were relegated from the top flight for the first time in 1936.

Jimmy Hogan was the man brought in to return Villa to the First Division which he achieved in 1938 but by the time football resumed after the Second World War he had ceded his position to Alex Massie. The former Villa captain consolidated the club as a First Division side but failed to win any trophies and left in August 1950 to be replaced by George Martin. The former Newcastle manager was also unable to bring any silverware to Villa Park but his successor, Eric Houghton (September 1953-November 1958),

ABOVE John Gregory cannot believe what he's seeing

OPPOSITE Jimmy Hogan (right), manager of Aston Villa, and Scott Duncan, manager of Ipswich Town, 1938

masterminded the 1957 FA victory that gave Villa their first trophy in nearly 40 years.

The 1960s saw a succession of managers including Joe Mercer, Dick Taylor, Tommy Cummings and Tommy Docherty among others before the arrival of Ron Saunders. After claiming the League title, Saunders left abruptly in February 1982 after a disagreement with the board and walked into the Birmingham City hotseat. Tony Barton managed the team to European Cup victory but found further success harder to come by and made way in July 1984 for short-lived managers such as Graham Turner, Billy McNeill and Josef Venglos.

The club has had some flamboyant leaders in the new Millennium including John Gregory, Graham Taylor, David O'Leary, Martin O'Neill, Gerard Houllier, Alex McLeish and Paul Lambert, the latter the club's 24th manager in their 133-year history.

McCann

MIDFIELDER GAVIN McCANN moved to Aston Villa in July 2003 for £2.25 million, two years after his one and only England cap in a game against Spain – ironically held at Villa Park in 2001.

Born in Blackpool on 10 January 1978, he first made a name for himself in the youth team at Everton before moving to Sunderland in 1998 for £500,000. While at Sunderland, the young player was part of the team who gained promotion to the Premiership in 1999.

McCann was David O'Leary's first major signing for Villa and he made his debut in a match against Portsmouth in August 2003. He was renowned for his combative and aggressive style in midfield, which over the years earned him a fair number of yellow cards. McCann was a committed and industrious part of the Villa team although he had a number of injury setbacks and at times came in for some criticism from fans.

He was transferred to Bolton Wanderers in June 2007 and made more than 30 appearances for the Lancashire side in what turned out to be a difficult campaign that saw them narrowly avoid relegation. Injury finally curtailed his career in 2011 and he has since had a number of coaching positions at lower league sides.

OPPOSITE David O'Leary endured a turbulent time in the Villa Park hotseat

ABOVE LEFT McCann was the subject of a £1 million transfer to Bolton Wanderers in June 2007

BELOW McCann challenges Liverpool's Xabi Alonso for the ball, 2007

McGrath

LIFE DIDN'T THROW ANY FAVOURS Paul McGrath's way when he was born. His Irish mother, terrified that her father would find out she was expecting a baby as the result of a relationship with a man from Nigeria, travelled to London to have her baby in secret. The young McGrath – Nwobilo, as was his name at the time – was brought up in a number of children's homes in Dublin. But this didn't stop the defender from becoming one of Ireland's first celebrities of mixed race.

The successful international, born on 4 December 1959, began his career in defence with St Patrick's Athletic in Dublin before signing for Manchester United in April 1982 for £30,000. He was 22 when he joined Ron Atkinson at Old Trafford where he contributed to nearly 200 first team games with his reliable and solid state of play. He gained an FA Cup winner's medal in 1985 and scored 16 goals during his time with Manchester United.

After seven years with the leading club he joined Aston Villa for £450,000 in August 1989 where he was to become

widely regarded as one of the greatest players to ever play for the club. The centre-back with dodgy knees who was allowed a less strenuous training regime proved he was reliable, controlled and good under pressure. His skills were instrumental to Villa when they beat McGrath's old team Manchester United in the League Cup final in 1994 – something he repeated two years later when the Villans beat Leeds United in 1996. In his 323 appearances for Villa he scored 10 goals.

McGrath moved to Derby County for a transfer fee of £100,000 in October 1996 and at the time he had already won 83 international caps for the Republic of Ireland. One fabulous event occurred during the World Cup 1994 when Ireland were drawn to play reigning champions Italy. Ireland were leading 1-0 when McGrath, who was marking Roberto Baggio, slid in front of his opponent. The ball was chipped into the air into the Irish player's face who then proceeded to chase the ball and deflate the Italians by denying them an equalising goal. McGrath had always been an integral part of the Irish team, particularly in the late 1980s and early 1990s under manager Jack Charlton. In 1993 he was voted the PFA Players' Player of the Year.

ABOVE Paul McGrath sees off the attentions of Ruel Fox in this 1994 match against Newcastle United

OPPOSITE McGrath defends against Manchester City, 1995

McGregor

THE IMPORTANCE OF WILLIAM McGregor to Aston Villa and to football in general cannot be stressed strongly enough. The Scottish draper, who was born in Perthshire in 1846, was a director of the club and founder of the Football League. He eventually became chairman of both the Football League and the Football Association and later was elevated to president of the Football League.

BELOW William McGregor, Football League president

Following his brother from Perthshire to Birmingham, McGregor's aim was to set up a drapery in his new town in 1879. He had been interested in football from an early age and quickly established himself at Calthorpe in the Midlands, but the lure of the strong Scottish influence at Aston Villa saw him join the club in 1877.

It was McGregor's organisational skills that saw Villa win their first trophy, the Birmingham Senior Cup in 1880 and by 1887 they had also won the FA Cup for the first time. Success at Villa and record attendances convinced the pioneering Scot that more should be done for competitive football and it was a letter from McGregor to other clubs in 1888 that got the ball rolling.

At an arranged meeting between the invited clubs it was decided to implement a League which began in September 1888. It was such a resounding success that a Second Division was introduced four years later. This exceptional man died in 1911 having realised his dreams.

Mellberg

SWEDISH DEFENDER OLOF Mellberg – born on 3 September 1977 – made his name playing in his native Sweden for Degerfors and AIK Solna between 1996 and 1999. His skills and talents took him to Spanish club Racing Santander, where he spent two seasons and made 97 appearances until the end of the 2000-01 season as the club were relegated.

Mellberg joined Aston Villa on 19 July 2001 for £5.6 million, where he made his debut on the opening day of the new season against Tottenham Hotspur. Despite missing a number of games during the 2001-02 season due to injury, the tall Swede has made a great impression at Villa Park and is now a firm favourite with the club and fans alike. His skills are continually developing and he proved his worth during Villa's 2002-03 campaign when he was a regular on the first team with his exceptional tackling skills. He had a strong campaign with Villa during 2003-04 and was equally impressive during the following season when he made 33

appearances for the club.

He suffered an untimely knee injury in April 2005 but returned for the 2005-06 season to continue his defence in Villa's back line. In January 2008, during a typically solid season, it was announced that Mellberg would be joining Juventus on a three-year contract. Mellberg, holder of more than 75 caps for Sweden did not bring any funds into Martin O'Neilll's kitty, however, as he left on a free transfer under the Bosman ruling.

Merson

DESPITE PERSONAL DIFFICULTIES, Paul Charles Merson, born in North London on 20 March 1968, had a prolific career as a forward, midfielder and manager. His influence on the game has been instrumental, while his popularity as a player was always high.

He began his career with Arsenal when he joined the club as an apprentice in 1984 and, after a spell on loan to Brentford, he made his debut for the Gunners against Manchester City in 1986. He was an integral part of the team at Arsenal during

BELOW Merson in action against Tottenham Hotspur, 2000

LEFT Merson clashes with Chris Makin of Ipswich, 2001

the late 1980s. The 1988-89 season was especially good for the young player who scored 10 goals, was voted the PFA Young Player of the Year and made his debut in the England Under-21s. In September 1991, he won his first full England cap when he appeared in a friendly against Germany.

He was in the Arsenal side that won the 1991 League Championship, the League Cup and FA Cup in 1993 and the Cup Winners' Cup a year later. Despite his success he found himself in difficulty when he publicly admitted to having a drink and drugs habit. The FA put him on a three-month rehabilitation programme and he returned to Arsenal in February 1995.

After a short spell with relegated Middlesbrough, Merson signed for Aston Villa in late 1998 for £6.75 million where his flamboyant style quickly established him as a firm favourite with the fans. He was instrumental in five good years with Villa – reaching the FA Cup final in 2000 – before he was given a free transfer to Portsmouth at the end of the 2001-02 season helping his new team reach the Premiership in 2002-03.

He wanted a move and jumped at the chance to join Walsall in 2003, however, his gambling habit was disrupting his career and he sought professional help. On his return he found himself in the manager's position. The 2004-05 campaign was difficult although 2005-06 looked brighter, but Merson was sacked in February 2006 as the team failed to avoid relegation. He resumed his playing career for a brief spell with Tamworth and announced he was retiring from professional football in March 2006. Today, Merson is a pundit for Sky Sports and writes a column for the *Arsenal FC* magazine.

Morley

TODAY, TONY MORLEY IS A flamboyant radio broadcaster on The Villan, but in his heyday on the pitch he was a successful winger who gave his best years to Aston Villa. Born William Anthony Morley in Ormskirk on 26 August 1954, he started his lifelong passion with football as an apprentice at Preston North End in July 1969. He became a professional in August 1972 and moved to Burnley in February 1976 on a £100,000 transfer. He joined Aston Villa for £200,000 in June three years later where he developed his "dangerous" skills under manager Ron Saunders.

He became renowned for his spectacular goals possibly his most memorable coming in a game against Everton at Goodison Park in the 1980-81 campaign...the goal was to win the winger the Goal of the Season award. That season was also memorable for Morley when he was an integral part of Villa's team that won the League Championship. The following year would see the Villans win the European Cup, again with a promising and steadfast Morley on the wing.

He established himself as a strong link in the Villa chain and scored a total of 34 goals from his 170 appearances for the club. He was renowned for his expert dribbles and crosses and was notoriously fast on the wing. His shots were powerful and he could use both feet which gave the young player an advantage. He was also part of the winning Villa side that claimed the European Super Cup in 1983.

Morley was transferred to rivals West Bromwich Albion during the 1983-84 campaign where his pace and stoic playing went down well. He was loaned to St Andrews in late 1984 before he moved to Japan to join FC Seiko in August 1985. The following year saw him move to Holland where he played for Den Hagg before joining Walsall in 1987 and Notts County before heading back to West Brom in August 1987.

After spells with a variety of clubs including Burnley (on loan October/ November 1988), Tampa Bay Rowdies in the US (1989), Sutton Coldfield Town (1992) he became a coach in both Australia and Hong Kong. Morley also assisted both Villa and WBA Old Stars during the 1990s. The devoted Villan won six caps for England but

LEFT Morley is now a regular on the Villa Old Stars circuit

OPPOSITE Morley on a run for Aston Villa, 1983

failed to be picked for any of the World Cup games in 1982 under manager Ron Greenwood. This seems bemusing since Greenwood was all in favour of attacking players and Morley had exactly what the manager needed.

Mortimer

TRUE ASTON VILLA LEGEND DENNIS
Mortimer must surely be one of the
all time greatest footballers who never
won a cap for England. Nothing is
really known about why this was the
case, but Dennis George Mortimer
(born in Liverpool on 5 April 1952)
was the stalwart and driving force at
Villa for 10 years.

His career began at Coventry City
where his promising midfield talents brought him to the
attention of Villa man-
ager Ron Saunders. He
joined Coventry City
as an apprentice in July
1967 and turned profes-
sional just over two years
later in September 1969.
Having worked his way
up through the ranks at
Coventry, Mortimer made
more than 200 appear-
ances for the club – 192
of them in the League –
where he found the back
of the net on 10 occasions.

He was signed for Villa
in December 1975 for
£175,000 where his passion and determination were developed to the full. His
outstanding skills were combined with
driving force and the will to win. He
was the backbone of the team between
1975 and 1985 and his 403 appearances
for the club saw him score 36 goals.
Mortimer found his niche between Des
Bremner and Gordon Cowans who
between them provided Villa with the
right attitude to seek and find glory in
the League Cup final in 1977. Further
success came in 1981 with the First

Division title while the European Cup and the European Super Cup were Villa's over the next two seasons. So impressive was Mortimer that Saunders was more than happy to give the captaincy to this exceptional midfielder. It was Mortimer that captained the side to glory in all three major victories.

He was loaned to Sheffield United in December 1984 and then moved to Brighton and Hove Albion in August 1985. Following his spell with Brighton, Mortimer made the controversial move to Birmingham City – Villa's archrivals – in August a year later before joining Kettering Town in July 1987. Redditch were pleased to snap him up as a player-manager between November 1987 and October 1988 while his next move took him to West Bromwich Albion as football in the community officer in August 1989. He later became the club's reserve team player and coach before he returned to the Villans as junior coach. Although not particularly fitting for a player of his stature, Mortimer did win six Under-21 caps for England as well as three B-team places and six Under-23 caps. Today, Mortimer is often heard on the club's radio station providing commentary on games.

Neal

BORN ON 3 APRIL 1932 IN COUNTY Durham, John Neal was at the height of his career as full-back with Aston Villa. It began for Neal as a professional in August 1949 when he signed for Hull City. In 1956 he joined King's Lynn but moved to Swindon Town in July 1957 where he took up the captaincy. Neal was signed for Aston Villa in July 1959 for £6,000 and it is here that his promising skills as full-back came to the fore.

As a replacement for Doug Winton, Neal was instrumental in Villa's Second Division title in 1960 and then again in winning the League Cup in 1961. He hung up his boots in June 1967 before taking over as manager of Wrexham following a stint as coach with the club in September 1968. Under Neal, Wrexham made it to the quarter-finals of the Cup Winners' Cup in 1972 but by 1974 his talents were shining as he repeated that feat in the FA Cup. He succeeded Jack Charlton at Middlesbrough and was then appointed manager at Chelsea in May 1981.

After a slow start he signed players such as David Speedie, Pat Nevin, Nigel Spackman and Kerry Dixon who helped the club to the top of the Second Division. Ill health saw Neal retire from the world of football in 1986.

Nicholl

CENTRE-HALF CHRISTOPHER JOHN Nicholl was born in Wilmslow, Cheshire on 12 October 1946. After learning his trade as an apprentice at Macclesfield Schools, he turned professional with Burnley in June 1963 but failed to make any League appearances for the club. In 1966 he moved to Witton Albion where he stayed for two years.

His natural flair took him to Halifax Town in 1968 where his 42 League appearances saw him score three goals for the club. Luton Town were next on Nicholl's list and he enjoyed three years, 97 League appearances and six goals before joining the Villans in March 1972 for £90,000. He made 210 League appearances for Villa, scoring 11 goals, and successfully captained the team to victory in the 1977 League Cup final over Everton. Perhaps Nicholl's most famous moment with Villa came in March 1976 when he single-handedly scored two goals for Villa and two own goals against Leicester City in a 2-2 draw. This must surely be unique!

He signed for Southampton in June 1977 and he registered eight goals for his new club during his 228 League appearances before joining Grimsby Town in August 1983. Nicholl won 51 caps for Northern Ireland where he regularly played alongside his cousin Jimmy Nicholl and has enjoyed managerial spells at Southampton and Walsall.

ABOVE LEFT Chris Nicholl celebrating with the League Cup after Villa's extra-time victory against Everton in 1977

ABOVE RIGHT Chris Nicholl was assistant manager of Northern Ireland for two years in the late 1990s

O'Neill

RIGHT Martin O'Neill during the Barclays Premiership match against Liverpool at Villa Park, 2007

AWARDED THE OBE IN 2004, Martin Hugh Michael O'Neill – born on 1 March 1952 in Kilrea, Northern Ireland – grew up playing Gaelic football and went on to become captain of his national team. His talents took him to Nottingham Forest from 1971 to 1981 where he made 285 League appearances scoring 48 goals from midfield.

Under manager Brian Clough, O'Neill was part of the team that saw Forest claim the First Division title in 1977-78, the League Cup in 1978 and 1979 and the European Cup on two occasions in 1979 and 1980. Between 1971 and 1984, O'Neill was also a key member of the Northern Ireland team, appearing 64 times for the national side where he netted the ball on eight occasions. However, in 1987, O'Neill hung up his boots and began what was to become a highly successful managerial career, initially at Grantham Town.

Following a short spell at Shepshed Charterhouse he joined Wycombe Wanderers in 1990. He stayed for five years and took them into the Football League as Conference champions three years later following which they were again promoted. O'Neill then made a move to Norwich City for pastures new but found his time at the club short-lived when he faced disagreements with chairman Robert Chase.

He left the club in December 1995 and was snapped up by Leicester City

ABOVE Martin O'Neill proudly holds up a Villa shirt as he is unveiled as manager in 2006

where he found things moved slowly to start with. However, after gaining promotion to the Premiership via the play-offs, things became successful at Leicester for O'Neill. In every season that O'Neill stayed as manager, the Premiership club finished in the top half of the table and won the Football League Cup in 1997. Two years later, the club reached the final again and, although on this occasion the trophy eluded them, they claimed victory again in 2000. These League Cup victories saw Leicester qualify for lucrative UEFA Cup runs.

He moved to become manager of Celtic in 2000 where his talents saw the club snatch victory in the Scottish League in 2001 and 2002 from rivals Rangers but he resigned in 2005 to take care of his wife who was suffering from cancer. In August 2006, O'Neill was appointed manager at Aston Villa and in his four years at the club, he can boast three successive top six finishes in the Premier League as well as a losing cup final appearance against Manchester United, the club's first in 10 years.

The club was rocked when he left five days before the start of the new season, allegedly over lack of funds for transfers, but he was soon back in work at Sunderland where he enjoyed a tempestuous couple of years. At the end of 2013, he was appointed Republic of Ireland manager with Roy Keane as his assistant.

Petrov

BELOW Stiliyan Petrov
skips away from
Hameur Bouazza of
Watford, 2007

STILIYAN PETROV – BETTER KNOWN to his teammates and fans as 'Stan' - is a living legend at the Villa, not only for his playing career at the club but because of his brave fight against cancer.

Born in Bulgaria, Petrov joined Celtic from CSKA Sofia in 1999 and stayed with the club until he moved to the Villa in 2006 along with his former manager Martin O'Neill. He later became club captain while also playing 106 matches for the Bulgarian national side.

Powerful and influential in the middle of the park, Petrov drove the team on week after week and he also scored his fair share of goals. He started his career at Villa as an anchorman - protecting the defence - in the central ground. But the 2011-12 saw him handed more license to thrill, as he did every week at Celtic - and Villa reaped the rewards.

In March 2012, Petrov was diagnosed with acute leukemia suspending his football career to have treatment. He announced his retirement from the game in May 2013.

Since retiring from playing, he has taken over as assistant coach of the Aston Villa Under-21 squad, working alongside another former Villa player, Gordon Cowans.

Platt

DAVID ANDREW PLATT WAS BORN on 10 June 1966 near Oldham in Lancashire and became one of Aston Villa's most prolific midfielders. He retired from the game in the late 1990s to coach Sampdoria in Serie A in Italy, before becoming player-coach at Nottingham Forest. Both jobs proved unsuccessful for Platt, and he eventually took up the job as the manager of the England Under-21 side. This resulted in a modicum of success and he left the side to become a football pundit in 2004. He is also a sports writer commenting on tactics for *FourFourTwo* magazine. However, it is his dazzling style on the pitch for which most hold him in high regard.

He joined Crewe Alexandra where he earned a solid reputation as a scoring midfielder. In his 134 League appearances at Crewe he scored 56 goals, a total he would almost match after his transfer to Aston Villa in 1988. Of the 121 League appearances for Villa he netted the ball no less than 50 times and he earned his first cap for England, under Bobby Robson, in 1989 in a friendly against Italy. Despite being a versatile and reliable player, he often found himself on the England bench initially. However, Platt was picked on occasions for England, and gave a particularly memorable performance in the

MIDDLE Steve Sidwell of Reading battles with Stiliyan Petrov, 2007

BELOW David Platt at full speed, 1990

ABOVE David Platt jumps to avoid Inter Milan keeper Walter Zenga

in the match against Belgium. Platt finished his England career in 1996 with a hefty 27 goals in 62 appearances that included 19 occasions when he captained his country.

Platt was an exceptional player for Villa during the early 1990s and captained the team providing leadership and inspiration and scored many goals from his position in midfield. In 1991 he left Villa for Italy where he joined Bari, Juventus and Sampdoria, but moved back to England four years later when he signed for Arsenal. Platt played with the London club for three years and was part of the 1998 Arsenal team that won the Premier League and FA Cup Double before his retirement in 1998. Platt served as manager of Sampdoria before leaving his post owing to poor results. Afterwards, he returned to England as player-manager of Nottingham Forest followed by a spell managing the England Under-21 team. He is now part of the management team at Manchester City.

World Cup 1990 when he started in a quarter-final tie against Cameroon. It was Platt who scored the opening goal in what was to be an exciting 3-2 victory for England after striking a superb volley

Quintessential Aston Villa
– the miscellaneous facts

BELOW David James celebrates breaking the record of clean sheets with Portsmouth's Linvoy Primus, April 2007

ASTON VILLA PLAYED ONE MATCH against rivals Small Heath in the 1870s that was so one-sided they won 22-0. One prankster even brought a chair out for goalkeeper George Copley to sit on.

Aston Villa caused an international stir on a tour of pre-World War II Germany when the team refused to give Adolf Hitler the Nazi salute. The German leader was unaccustomed to such an insult as other British teams had complied.

Portsmouth goalkeeper David James created history on 22 April 2007 when he prevented the opposition from

scoring for a record 142nd time in the Premiership. Ironically, this record came in a match against Aston Villa for whom James played 69 League games between 1999 and 2001.

The 1930-31 season saw Aston Villa set a record of 128 League goals scored and they succeeded to find the net in each of their home games. Despite this scoring feat, they could only finish as runners-up to Arsenal. Winger Eric Houghton registered a more than respectable tally of 30 goals but found himself second in the club's scoring lists behind Tom "Pongo" Waring. The Birkenhead-born striker smashed plenty of records during his five years at Villa Park, averaging more than two goals in every three games.

Rimmer

JOHN JAMES RIMMER – BORN ON 10 February in Southport, Lancashire – is the only English footballer to have won a European Cup winner's medal at two different clubs, which is even more amazing when it is considered that Rimmer actually only spent nine minutes on the pitch over the two matches. He was an unused substitute in 1968 when Manchester United beat Benfica and had to leave the pitch injured in 1982.

Jimmy Rimmer's career began in the youth team for Manchester United in 1963 and he turned professional for the club two years later. He made 34 League appearances at Old Trafford before signing with Arsenal in 1974. However, Rimmer found his opportunities limited after Terry Neill had brought in Pat Jennings and was happy to move to Villa Park in 1977.

It is probably his time at Aston Villa, however, for which he is best remembered on the pitch. He was the first choice keeper for a total of six seasons and made 146 appearances for the club – 124 of them in the League – and won a First Division winner's medal in 1981. While at Manchester United, Rimmer had been on loan to Swansea City during 1973 and he returned there in 1983. He was at the club for three years before his retirement in 1986.

ABOVE After hanging up his boots, Jimmy Rimmer worked as a goalkeeping coach in China and Canada

Samuel

RIGHT Samuel
challenges for the ball

BELOW Samuel
during a match against
Arsenal, 2006

SAMUEL SIGNED FOR ASTON VILLA in 1998 and, though often nervous on the pitch, became one of the best left backs in the country while at the club.

The defender, who was born Jlloyd Samuel on 29 March 1981 in Trinidad and Tobago, worked his way up to the professional game from St Joseph's Academy in London before joining Charlton Athletic's youth team.

He made his debut for Villa in September 1999 in a 5-0 League Cup victory over Chester City. He was disappointed though when he missed a call up to the 2002 European Under-21s Championships due to a groin injury. Renowned for being nervous on the pitch, Graham Taylor's managerial style helped the youngster to develop and he enjoyed his best season with the club under David O'Leary in 2003-04. It helped establish Samuel as one of the leading left-backs in the Premiership and he was rewarded with a place on the England team in a friendly against Sweden in March 2004 (although he remained an unused substitute despite eight players being replaced). The reliable defender made an application to play for Trinidad and Tobago after he failed to win an England place.

As the 2006-07 season drew to an end he eventually signed with Bolton and now plays for Iranian side, Esteghlal, as well as his national team.

Saunders, Dean

PROLIFIC WELSH STRIKER DEAN Saunders today enjoys a career as a BBC pundit, and is also currently without a club to coach. He was a huge hit at Aston Villa, the seventh senior club that he joined during his varied career which began in the youth team for Swansea City in 1980. He turned professional for the club in 1982 and had spells at Cardiff City (on loan), Brighton and Hove Albion (1985-1987), Oxford United (1987-1988), Derby County (1988-1991) and Liverpool (1991-1992)

before he signed for Villa in 1992 in a deal that cost the club £2.5 million.

He made 110 League appearances for the Villans and scored 37 goals. He was a big favourite with the fans and established a strong and reliable partnership with Dalian Atkinson where the first season of the newly created Premiership saw the club finish in second place. Saunders was instrumental, despite the team's recent lack of form during the 1993-94 season, in claiming victory in the League Cup over rivals Manchester United. He scored 15 League goals the following season, signed for Galatasaray in 1995 under Graeme Souness before spells at Nottingham Forest, Sheffield United, Benfica and Bradford City. The Welshman won 75 caps for his national side and scored 22 goals.

ABOVE Saunders celebrates scoring in 1994

LEFT Saunders chases Andy Sinton of Sheffield Wednesday, 1994

Saunders, Ron

BORN IN BIRKENHEAD ON 6 November 1932, Ron Saunders began his football career as a hard-hitting centre-forward at Everton, Gillingham, Portsmouth, Watford and Charlton

scoring more than 200 goals during his 13-year illustrious career on the pitch. Solid, dependable and extremely adept at hitting the back of the net, Saunders was the top goalscorer for his third club, Portsmouth, for six consecutive seasons, helping his side claim the Third Division Championship in 1962. Even today, Saunders is Pompey's third highest goal scorer, but he hung up his boots in 1967 while with his final club, Charlton Athletic.

Despite his prolific career as a centre-forward, it was as a high-profile manager that Saunders was to find his niche. He began his "second" football career with Yeovil Town in 1967 and stayed for two years before taking over the reins at Oxford United (1969). He joined Second Division Norwich who went on to win the title in 1972 – the first time the club had achieved this. Saunders left the club in 1973 and headed for Manchester City however, it was his move to Aston Villa where he succeeded Vic Crowe in 1974 that was to stamp his name on the football managers' map.

For eight years, Saunders' influence saw the team flourish, especially with help from assistant Tony Barton later in his career, and he steered his club to the League Cup final in both 1975 and 1977. However, the club were to claim the First Division in 1981 when they won the title for the first time in 71 years under Saunders' guidance. Sadly, in 1982, a disagreement over his contract with the Villa board saw Saunders resign and it came just as Villa were about to claim their greatest achievement – the European Cup. Controversially, he headed straight for archrivals, Birmingham City, who were relegated in 1984. Under Saunders, the team were back in Division One the following season but in 1986, Saunders left the club for pastures new. He took on struggling West Bromwich Albion who slid into the Second Division. A year later with no success at promotion, Saunders was sacked.

In December 2006, he was invited to Villa Park as guest of honour by new chairman Randy Lerner for a match between the Villans and Manchester United.

LEFT Ron Saunders (r) watches his team play, 1977

Shaw

THE EARLY 1980S SAW STRIKER GARY Shaw's explosive style of play burst onto the scene at Aston Villa. Born on

21 January 1961 in Birmingham, the promising forward began his football career with the club as an apprentice in July 1977 making his debut in a game against Bristol City in August 1978.

He turned professional in 1979 and struck up a fabulous partnership for the Villans with Peter Withe, managing to find the back of the net on 20 occasions during the 1980-81 season. Shaw was voted PFA Young Player of the Year in 1981 in a season that saw Villa claim the League Championship. The following season saw the sensational striker's form continue as he scored 14 times adding 24 the following season. He was an integral part of the Villa side that won both the European Cup (1982) and the European Super Cup (1983). The former resulted in Shaw being named the European Cup's Player of the Year but the fairytale was not to last.

Shaw suffered a serious knee injury during the 1983-84 campaign which was to effectively end his career. He underwent a staggering six operations to rectify the problem, but his promising start at Villa was over. He tried his luck abroad following the surgery and moved first to Copenhagen and then Klagenfurt in Austria upon leav-

ing Villa Park at the end of the 1987-88 season. Shaw failed to make any League appearances for either club and returned to England and a short spell with Walsall in 1990. The same year saw him try his luck with Kilmarnock where his four League appearances resulted in no goals.

He joined Shrewsbury Town later that same year and over the following season made 22 League appearances which saw him score on five occasions for the club. Finding the stress on his knee too great, Shaw retired from football in 1991. He was just 30 years old.

Earlier in his career when his goalscoring was prolific, Shaw had come to the attention of the England Under-21 squad, winning seven caps. Although he never won a full cap for England, he did win nine Youth caps.

LEFT Although he was included in the preliminary England squad for the 1982 World Cup, he was eliminated from the final 22

ABOVE Sorensen points orders during a Barclays Premiership match against Bolton Wanderers, 2007

RIGHT Sorensen denies Emmanuel Adebayor of Arsenal, 2006

Sorensen

GOALKEEPER THOMAS SORENSEN signed for Aston Villa in August 2003 in a deal costing the club £2.25 million. Born in Odense, Denmark on 12 June 1976, at 6' 4", the tall Dane cuts an imposing figure for opposing attackers. He joined Villa from relegated Sunderland and was part of David O'Leary's dreams for the club.

Sorensen's skills have given the keeper one of the best reputations in the Premiership and his decision to move to Sunderland instead of to Ajax or Udinese before signing for Villa gave him a regular international place. His ambition was to replace fellow Dane Peter Schmeichel in the international goal – he achieved it with grace and soon became the Danish favourite.

His first season at Villa looked promising despite the lack of big wins. The Dane's debut came for the Villans in a match against Portsmouth at the start of the 2003-04 season. He was a success with the club and fans alike and was an important part of the team that changed Villa's fortunes in the 2004-05 season. His impressive form has earned the keeper more than 70 caps at international level and he was his country's first choice keeper during Euro 2004. Having lost his number one jersey to Scott Carson, Villa decided not to renew Sorensen's contract and the Dane was released at the end of the 2007-08 campaign without having made a single appearance that season.

Southgate

GARETH SOUTHGATE HAD AN illustrious league career and played nearly 200 times for the Villa. He has been manager of the England Under-21 team since August 2013.

He won the League Cup in his first season with Villa in 1995-96 which also meant they qualified for the UEFA Cup. Southgate played in every Premier League game during the 1998–99 season. He continued to play for Villa in the 1999–2000 season as Villa reached the FA Cup Final but handed in a transfer request just before Euro 2000 claiming that "if I am to achieve in my career, it is time to move on " which didn't endear him to the faithfull!

He made 57 appearances for England featuring in the 1998 World Cup and both the1996 and 2000 European Championships. His playing career ended in May 2006 at the age of 35, and after more than 500 league appearances, he was appointed Middlesbrough manager, a position held until 2009 prior to the present England job.

Spink

ANOTHER HIGHLY REGARDED former goalkeeper for Aston Villa was Nigel Spink. He began his career in the youth teams of West Ham United in 1976 and Chelmsford City (1976-77) before signing for the Villans in January 1977 for £4,000.

RIGHT Spink is drenched during a thunderstorm at the San Siro in Milan, 1994

BELOW Spink in action during the 1995 FA Cup

Born Nigel Philip Spink in Chelmsford on 8 August 1958, the keeper waited five years at Villa for his "big break" which came in the European Cup final in 1982. Regular keeper Jimmy Rimmer was injured in the ninth minute of the game against Bayern Munich and Spink's big chance had arrived. He made the game his own, kept a clean sheet and the Villa won the final 1-0. It was to be the second of 460 appearances that Spink would make in the first-team.

He remained dedicated to the Villans for almost two decades but 1996 saw the Villa Park stalwart head for West Bromwich Albion where he stayed for a year. Millwall (1997-2000) was his next stop before he signed for Forest Green Rovers in 2000. He made 14 appearances for his final club before hanging up his boots in 2001.

Spink's excellent reputation on the pitch was well-founded. He was a good shot-stopper and at 6' 2" was always calm and prepared for any challenge the opposition could kick or head at him. His confident style combined with his courage and sound anticipation made him a firm Villa favourite.

Staunton

STEVE STAUNTON WAS SPOTTED playing for Dundalk in Ireland at the age of 17 by Liverpool scouts and was signed for the club that same year in 1986 by manager Kenny Dalglish. At a fee of £20,000 Staunton – born in Drogheda, Ireland on 19 January 1969 – was a bargain and he worked his way up through the Liverpool reserves during his first two seasons.

He was on loan to Bradford City during the 1987-88 season for a short spell but was back at Liverpool to make his debut as a defender in September 1988 in a 1-1 draw with Tottenham at Anfield. His impressive performance that day earned him a regular spot in the first team for the remainder of the season. He even scored a goal on his second outing for the club.

When tragedy struck at Hillsborough on 15 April 1989, Staunton was known to have comforted many bereaved families and attended a number of funerals following the fateful event. The semi-final of the FA Cup just one month later saw a promising Staunton put in a magical performance in Liverpool's 3-1

ABOVE Staunton during the 1994 UEFA Cup first round tie against Inter Milan

victory over Nottingham Forest.

Due to his continued form and formidable presence on the pitch for Liverpool it came as a surprise when the club transferred him to Aston Villa in August 1991 for £1.1 million. It has been argued that Graeme Souness wanted rid of Staunton because his Irish heritage meant that the new manager of Liverpool had too many non-English team members for European

ties. Thankfully, such ridiculous rulings have been abolished with the Bosman ruling which states that there are no longer quotas for EU citizens on teams in member countries.

However, that wasn't much use to Staunton who made his debut with Villa in August 1991 in a 3-2 victory over Sheffield Wednesday. His time at Villa saw him win League Cup winner's medals in 1994 and 1996. He failed to win any further medals with Villa but returned to Anfield in 1998 under the Bosman ruling. He stayed two years before moving to Coventry City and Walsall.

His international career was just as impressive as his domestic one with 102 appearances for Eire and Staunton moved into management in the 2000s. He was appointed Villa's reserve team coach before taking up the reins of the Irish international side in January 2006. This role lasted until October 2007 when Staunton paid the price for Ireland's failure to qualify for Euro 2008 but he joined Leeds United in February 2008 as assistant manager and more recently has managed at Darlington.

justice in defence, midfield and attack and is an extremely physical footballer who has gained a reputation as a prolific goalscorer. He was the Premiership's top goalscorer during the 1997-98 season alongside Coventry City's Dion Dublin and Liverpool's Michael Owen.

He joined Norwich City in 1991 as centre-half before becoming a striker. It was a move that paid off for both Sutton and his club as the 1992-93 season saw Norwich lead the Premiership – they finished in third place overall. He moved to Blackburn Rovers in 1994 for the phenomenal fee of £5 million, making him the most expensive player in English football at the time. At Ewood Park he established a striving partnership with Alan Shearer scoring 15 goals in the Premiership which gave Blackburn their first League title since 1914.

But things started going adrift for the striker in the 1995-96 season when he was plagued by injury and suffered

LEFT Chris Sutton and Kevin Davies of Bolton Wanderers compete for the ball, 2006

Sutton

STRIKER AND CENTRAL DEFENDER Chris Sutton began his time at Aston Villa in October 2006 having followed Martin O'Neill from Celtic. Born on 10 March 1973 in Nottingham, Christopher Roy Sutton is able to do

a loss of form. The following year saw his fitness return and he won a cap for England in 1997. Blackburn Rovers suffered relegation at the end of the 1998-99 campaign and Sutton was sold to Chelsea for £10 million where he stayed for a year. It was not a happy time for Sutton who struggled with almost every aspect of the Chelsea game. He moved to Celtic in 2000 for £6 million.

Here he broke the record for the quickest goal scored in a match against archrivals Rangers – it took him just 18 seconds to find the back of the net and he was voted SPFA Player of the Year for 2003-04. On 3 October 2006, Sutton signed for Villa to play until the end of the 2006-07 season. He rejoined his former Celtic boss Martin O'Neill and scored his first goal for his new employers on 11 November that same year.

December brought difficulties for Sutton, however, when he suffered blurred vision in a game against Manchester United. Despite seeing several specialists, the problem was persistent so Sutton announced his decision to retire from professional football in July 2007. He finished his career at the age of 34 with an impressive tally of 151 goals in 410 league games.

Taylor

TODAY, GRAHAM TAYLOR IS A pundit on the BBC's Radio Five Live while his last job as a manager was with Aston Villa between 2002 and 2003. Taylor came out of retirement especially to take over the reins at Villa Park – a job he undertook for the second time – but decided to retire from management for good at the end of the 2002-03 season when Villa finished in 16th place in the Premiership. There were tensions between Taylor and club chairman Doug Ellis, with the experienced former England manager wanting a complete overhaul so that the club could become more competitive.

It was not the first time that Taylor had managed the same club on two separate occasions. In fact, he managed Watford on three occasions. He first went to Watford in 1977 and stayed until 1987 and then returned in

1996 before finally managing the team between 1997 and 2001. Sir Elton John bought Watford in 1996 for the second time and wanted Taylor on his staff at Vicarage Road. He joined as general manager and appointed himself manager a year later winning the Division Two Championship.

ABOVE Graham Taylor watches his side at Villa Park, 2002

OPPOSITE Sutton on his Aston Villa debut in 2006

The club won promotion to the Premiership the following season but were relegated in the next campaign. When Watford finished ninth in Division One at the end of the 2000-2001 season Taylor retired for the first time. His management career began with

Lincoln City where he was the youngest FA coach to be appointed aged just 27. He then became manager – again the youngest at 28 – in December 1972.

Next came his first stint at Watford where he was hired – for the first time by pop legend Elton John – astutely as it turns out. Taylor took the Fourth Division team to the First Division in just five years. Watford also made it to the third round of the UEFA Cup under Taylor and finished the top division in second place at the end of the 1982-83 campaign. With Taylor's guidance, Watford made it to the FA Cup final against Everton in 1984 but were defeated 2-0.

Born on 15 September 1944 in Worksop, Nottinghamshire, Taylor then joined relegated Aston Villa in 1987. The Villans soon found themselves back in Division One and success with Villa gave Taylor the job of manager with England in 1990. He remained manager for three years but gave up his post when England failed to qualify for the World Cup in 1994. Prior to management, Taylor played for Grimsby Town (1962-1968) and Lincoln City (1968-1972) however a serious hip injury saw him retire from the game.

Townsend

TELEVISION PUNDIT ANDY Townsend was born in Maidstone on 23 July 1963. He began his career with Welling United youth team in 1980 and remained dedicated to the club for four years before turning professional and signing for Weymouth in 1984.

The midfielder moved to Southampton a year later where he made 71 League appearances and scored a total of eight goals. He was signed by Lawrie McMenemy for £35,000 and made his debut against Aston Villa in April 1985. Chris Nicholl took over the helm at Southampton and Townsend found himself in and out of the team but disaster struck when in a friendly against his former club Weymouth, Townsend broke his leg in 1986. By January 1987 he was back in the first team having regained his fitness and he became a regular alongside Glenn Cockerill and Jimmy Case in midfield.

Nicholl sold Townsend to Norwich City for £300,000 in August 1988 where he remained until 1990 when he moved to Chelsea. But it was his success at Norwich that earned Townsend a place

ABOVE Andy Townsend beats Steve Talboys of Wimbledon to the ball, 1994

Just a year earlier in July 1993, in a transfer of just over £2 million, the midfielder moved to Villa. Villa went on to win the Coca-Cola Cup final against Manchester United in 1994 and Townsend then captained the winning team when the Villans claimed the trophy in a 3-0 win over Leeds United two years later. He made 134 League appearances for Villa and netted the ball on eight occasions.

He joined Middlesbrough in August 1997 for £500,000 and made 37 appearances for his new club while Boro won promotion in to the Premiership. He established a steady partnership with Paul Gascoigne in the 1998-99 campaign but the following season saw him fighting for a place in the first team. In 1999 he transferred to West Bromwich Albion where he made 17 League appearances. Disappointingly for Townsend a persistent knee injury meant the end of his playing days and he retired from professional football in July 2000. He is now a regular television pundit.

in the Republic of Ireland's international squad and he made his debut in 1989 against France. By 1994 he took over the captaincy of the international team for the World Cup.

UEFA Cup

ASTON VILLA HAVE QUALIFIED for the UEFA Cup on 10 occasions but the furthest they have ever progressed in the competition is when they reached the quarter-finals in 1977-78 and again 20 years later.

Fenerbahce were easily disposed of 4-0 at home and 2-0 away in 1977-78 before a second round encounter with Gornik Zabrze. A 2-0 victory over the Polish side in the home leg with two goals from Ken McNaught ensured Villa's survival in the competition despite being held 1-1 in the return fixture. Atletico Bilbao were their third round opponents and an aggregate 3-1 victory set up a mouthwatering tie with Barcelona. The Spanish giants boasted Johann Cruyff in their line-up and it was the Dutchman who opened the scoring. When Barcelona added a second it seemed as if Villa were on their way out but goals from McNaught and John

Deehan levelled the tie. The return match saw John Gidman sent off for retaliation before Villa took the lead through Brian Little. The 10 men could not hold out though and Barcelona scored twice to win through to the semi-finals.

BELOW The Aston Villa team warm up during a training session before the UEFA Cup second round first leg match against Celta Vigo, 1998

Goals from Ian Taylor and Dwight Yorke gave the home side a 2-1 victory in the second leg to set up a third round clash with Steaua Bucharest.

Villa went down 2-1 in Romania despite Yorke again getting his name on the scoresheet but it was Milosevic and Taylor who rescued their team's hopes at Villa Park. They struck to register a 2-0 victory that put Villa into the quarter-finals for the second time where their opponents were Atletico Madrid. The Spaniards drew first blood and hung on to take a 1-0 advantage to Villa Park where goals from Taylor and Stan Collymore gave the home side a 2-2 draw on aggregate but it was the visitors who progressed to a semi-final meeting with Lazio courtesy of the away goal rule.

Villa have suffered second round exits against Spartak Moscow (4-3 on aggregate in 1983-84), Inter Milan (3-2 in 1990-91), Deportivo La Coruna (2-1 in 1993-94), Trabzonspor (2-2 in 1994-95 but Villa went out on away goals) and Celta Vigo (3-2 in 1998-99). All their other campaigns have come to an abrupt end in the first round against Antwerp (5-1 in 1975-76), Helsingsborgs (1-1 in 1996-97 on away goals) and NK Varteks (3-3 in 2001-02, again on away goals).

The 1997-98 campaign kicked off with a 0-0 draw in Bordeaux and Savo Milosevic scored the only goal of the return fixture in front of 33,000 at Villa Park. The second round saw them pitted against Athletico Bilbao and the Villa defence once again proved an impenetrable barrier in the away leg.

Vassell

IT WAS DARIUS VASSELL'S RECORD-breaking 1996-97 season in the Aston Villa youth team when he scored 39 goals that really brought him to the attention of the Villa Park hierarchy. Vassell was born on 13 June 1980 in Sutton Coldfield to Jamaican parents and made his Premiership debut as a substitute for Julian Joachim in August 1998 when given a chance by manager John Gregory in the 3-1 win against Middlesbrough.

He made another substitute appearance in the UEFA Cup on 15 September and could not have had a more fantastic European debut. Norwegian side Stromsgodset were winning 2-1 at Villa Park and Vassell got his chance with 10 minutes of normal time remaining. He scored his first ever top class goal for Villa in the first minute of injury time to level the tie and then unbelievably

netted the winner after 94 minutes. It immediately endeared him to Villa fans but it took him until 3 February 2001, however, to find his scoring touch in a League game. Again he netted a brace as Villa won 3-0 at Bradford City.

The 2001-02 campaign saw Vassell strike up a formidable partnership with Juan Pablo Angel that sent Villa temporarily to the top of the Premiership.

ABOVE Darius Vassell on the run, 1998

ABOVE Vassell scores a late winning goal during the UEFA Cup against Stromsgodset at Villa Park, 1998

It brought the youngster to the attention of England manager Sven Goran Eriksson and Vassell made his England debut in a friendly against Holland. Vassell started the match and scored his country's equaliser after 61 minutes to give a final result of 1-1. It was the start of a tumultuous two-year period for Vassell who went on to star in another 21 internationals (scoring five more goals) before his England career halted in June 2004 when he missed the final spot kick in the Euros and England were knocked out by Portugal.

His greatest asset was his pace and he tormented defenders by running at them with the ball. It was a tactic he has used to great effect and he had scored 42 goals in 167 League appearances by the time he left Villa Park in July 2005. Manchester City paid £2million for his services and he enjoyed a fruitful partnership with Andy Cole. Vassell went on to play for Turkish side Ankaragucu as well as Leicester City but a serious knee injury eventually forced his retirement in 2011.

Villa Cross Wesleyan Chapel

ASTON VILLA CAN TRACE ITS origins back to a meeting held by members of the local Villa Cross Wesleyan Chapel Methodist cricket team under a flickering gas lamp on Heathfield Road in Birmingham. They had witnessed a game on a nearby meadow and wanted an alternative pursuit during the winter after the cricket season had come to a close. So it was that Aston Villa – the team allegedly taking their name from a local mansion – was founded in 1874.

With football in its infancy, Villa played their first match against Aston Brook St Mary's rugby club and the fixture was truly a game of two halves. The first was played under rugby rules while those of football were observed after the interval with Villa winning 1-0.

The development of the club had a particularly Scottish flavour, largely because of the workforce who were attracted to Birmingham's growing industry. George Ramsay, in particular,

LEFT George Ramsay was allegedly the last person to kick a ball at Perry Barr and the first to kick one at Villa Park

played a pivotal role in Villa's early years after moving to the area as a 21-year-old looking for work. He joined the club after watching a training session in a local park and – having played first-class football in his native country – took on role of trainer as well as player. He was also instrumental in organising the club's first proper home ground of Perry Barr.

Villa Park

ASTON VILLA USED VARIOUS grounds including Aston Park, Wellington Road and Perry Barr before settling at Villa Park in 1897. Indeed, they also played home games at Aston Lower Grounds, a Victorian amusement park that would in the very near future become transformed into Villa

BELOW The main entrance to Villa Park, home of Aston Villa

Park. The club had settled at Perry Barr in 1876 but found that they needed a larger home as the team's popularity grew and they succeeded on the pitch.

In fact, when Villa entertained Preston North End in the fifth round of the 1887-88 FA Cup more than 27,000 spectators turned up to watch the match. As kick-off time approached, the police realised that they didn't have enough manpower on duty to control the crowd and they had to call on soldiers stationed nearby to help restore order after spectators wanting to get a better view had twice encroached on the pitch. The playing surface had been destroyed by the crowd and the mounted police so the two team captains agreed to play the match as a friendly which the visitors won 3-1. However, the FA later backed Preston's claim to victory, citing that Villa could not replay the game as it was their fault they couldn't maintain order.

So it was that Villa spent £20,000 on a new ground which they named Villa Park. The 70,000 capacity stadium was the pride of Birmingham and the first game to be played there was a League fixture against Blackburn Rovers. The home fans went home in buoyant spirits having seen their side win 3-0.

SPACE TO LET

Villa Park has seen plenty of redevelopment over the years with the cycle track being removed in 1914 so that the Witton Lane Stand could be enlarged and the famous Holte End banking – named after the owner of Aston Hall to whom the land had previously belonged – was completed at the end of 1939. But it was the decision to use Villa Park as a venue for the 1966 World Cup that brought major transformation with the pitch being extended, the Witton Lane Stand being made all-seater and seats being introduced to the Witton End banking.

The North Stand was built in the late 1970s while the Witton Lane Stand was rebuilt two decades later and renamed the Doug Ellis Stand. The new millennium saw the completion of a new Trinity Road Stand (which replaced the structure built in the 1920s) and the club has initial planning permission to rebuild the North Stand in the same style as the Trinity Road Stand. When completed, the capacity of Villa Park will increase to around 50,000.

Waring

W

RIGHT Tom 'Pongo' Waring (l) is beaten to a header by Tottenham Hotspur's Fred Channell

BELOW Pongo Waring earned the nickname "Gay Cavalier" for his scoring exploits during 1930-31

TO DESCRIBE TOM WARING AS AN enigma is an understatement to say the least. Villa's record goalscorer with 49 League goals in the 1930-31 season had his own dressing room and was a law unto himself, turning up for training when he wanted but the Villa Park faithful loved him because he was a scoring machine. In a total of 226 appearances he found the back of the net on 167 occasions...an incredible record of consistency.

Nicknamed "Pongo" after a popular cartoon of the interwar years, Waring – born in Birkenhead on 12 October 1906 – joined Villa from Tranmere Rovers for the princely sum of £4,700 in February 1928. His five-year spell at Villa wrote his name in the record books and he is probably the greatest striker ever to have worn the claret and blue shirt.

Waring joined Barnsley in November

1935 and the move angered fans so much that thousands of them demanded for his return but to no avail. He also played for Wolves, Tranmere (again), Accrington Stanley, Bath City, Ellesmere Port Town, Graysons FC, Birkenhead Dockers and Harrowby before guesting for New Brighton as the Second World War began. He was capped five times by England (scoring four goals) between 1931 and 1932.

Waring worked for the Hercules Motor and Cycle Company in Aston following his retirement and died on 20 December 1980.

Whittingham

GUY WHITTINGHAM ARRIVED AT Villa Park in 1993 with the expectation of the Villa Park faithful on his shoulders. The striker – born in Evesham on 10 November 1964 – had just enjoyed a record-breaking season at Portsmouth where he netted a record 42 League goals as the Fratton Park outfit narrowly missed out on an automatic promotion slot by goal difference. Bought by Villa for £1.2 million (it had only cost Pompey £450 to buy him out of the Army in 1989!), it was hoped that he could carry on in the same vein.

Sadly things did not work out and although he scored five League goals in 25 appearances for the Villans he found himself sent out on loan to Championship side Wolves. Whittingham was transferred to Sheffield Wednesday in 1994 for £700,000 and enjoyed a successful five years there playing 113 times and scoring 22 League goals. He then found himself farmed out to Wolves (again), Watford and Portsmouth where he scored seven goals in nine League appearances. That persuaded Pompey manager Alan Ball to bring him back to Fratton Park before

he hung up his boots in 2001 after a short spell at Wycombe Wanderers. He has had various positions in non-League management and latterly was appointed assistant manager at Crawley Town in December 2013.

BELOW Guy Whittingham keeps a close eye on Everton's Joe Parkinson in a goalless match in March 1994

ABOVE Peter Withe scores the winning goal in the European Cup final against Bayern Munich

Withe

JOURNEYMAN STRIKER PETER Withe (born in Liverpool on 30 August 1951) had played for nine clubs before he arrived at Villa Park in 1980 as the club's record signing at a cost of £500,000. He is probably best remembered for scoring the most important goal in the history of Aston Villa when he bundled the ball into the net for the only goal of the 1982 European Cup final. Gary Shaw's turn had been too intricate for the Bayern Munich defence and Tony Morley fired a low cross across the face of the goal from the resulting pass. Withe tried to side-foot the ball into the net but it bobbled and went in off his shin and Villa were crowned kings of Europe.

Withe stayed with Villa for five years and scored a more than respectable 74 goals in 182 League appearances, helping the Villans to their first League title in more than 70 years in 1980-81. He was capped 11 times by England between 1981 and 1984 and scored just once, against Hungary in a 2-0 win in April 1983. He also became the first Villa player to feature in an England World Cup squad when he was selected for the 1982 tournament in Spain.

It was a far cry from his early career when he had played for Southport and Barrow before spells trying his luck in South Africa (with Port Elizabeth City and Arcadia Shepards) and America (Portland Timbers) these were sandwiched by a period in the First Division with Wolverhampton Wanderers. He moved from there to Birmingham City where he scored nine goals in 35 League games before signing with Nottingham Forest shortly after the start of the 1976-77 season. There he made an immediate impact scoring 16 times as Forest returned to the top flight and 12 months later they had won the First Division title.

Once more, Withe was transferred at the start of a new season and after just one game of the 1978-79 campaign he moved to Newcastle United where he scored 25 goals in 76 League games.

On his release from Aston Villa, Withe spent four years with Sheffield United (including a loan spell at Birmingham City) and finished his playing career with Huddersfield Town in 1990.

Withe returned to Villa Park as assistant manager to Josef Venglos before embarking on a managerial career of his own that has included stints at Wimbledon and in charge of the Thailand and Indonesian national teams.

ABOVE Peter Withe on international duty, 1982

Wright

THE SHORTEST PLAYER IN THE history of the Premiership at just 5' 4" tall, Alan Wright signed for Villa in March 1995 and went straight into a team that was struggling at the wrong end of the table. Villa had endured a torrid first half of the season, winning just three of their opening 23 games. Wright (born on 28 September 1971 in Ashton-under-Lyne) registered eight appearances until the end of the campaign as his new club managed to finish just two places and five points above the relegation zone.

Wright had started his career as a trainee with Blackpool in 1989 and went on to make 98 appearances for the Bloomfield Road outfit before a £400,000 transfer to Blackburn Rovers. He joined the Ewood Park club at the right time: Jack Walker had just taken over and was spending millions bringing in Kenny Dalglish as manager and players of the calibre of Alan Shearer and Chris Sutton. The SAS strike partnership powered Blackburn to the Premiership title in 1994-95 but Wright found himself surplus to requirements with the emergence of Graeme Le Saux.

Alan Wright found himself a major component of a Villa side that consistently finished in the top half of the Premiership and was ever-present during the 1995-96 campaign that saw the Villans claim the League Cup. The left-

back went on to register an impressive 261 League appearances for the Villa Park outfit and scored five goals. Two of those strikes came in the space of five games during the 1995-96 season, away to Middlesbrough on New Year's Day and at home to Leeds United just over a month later.

After being released on a free transfer in August 2003, he signed for Middlesbrough but played just twice before being sent out on loan to Sheffield United two months later. He made that move permanent in January 2004 and went on to make 33 appearances for his new club before again finding himself surplus to requirements and being sent out on loan (to Derby County, Leeds United, Cardiff City, Doncaster Rovers and Nottingham Forest). He was, however, part of the side that knocked Aston Villa out of the third round of the 2004-05 FA Cup with a 3-1 victory at Bramall Lane. Gareth Barry had put the visitors 1-0 up shortly after the interval but the home team hit back with three goals to send the Premiership side home disappointed.

ABOVE Wright was signed for £1 million in the summer of 1995

X-tra Time

VILLA SEEM TO ENJOY MORE LUCK in extra-time and penalty shootouts than other teams but they were fortunate to progress to the 2000 League Cup semi-final. With their fifth round match against West Ham United tied at 2-2 after extra-time, the two sides faced the nerve-racking scenario of penalties and it was the Hammers who showed their mettle by winning 5-4. Fortunately for Villa, the London club were found guilty of fielding an ineligible player and the match was ordered to be replayed. Villa triumphed 3-1 in the rematch to set up a semi-final meeting with Leicester City but were unable to penetrate the Foxes' defence and lost 1-0 on aggregate.

The 1977 League Cup proved to be an elongated affair as it took Villa three matches to get past both Queens Park Rangers and Everton. The semi-final

against QPR saw two draws (0-0 and 2-2) before the Midlanders won 3-0 at Highbury while the final itself again saw two draws (0-0 and 1-1) before Villa won 3-2 after extra-time at Old Trafford.

That pales into insignificance to the marathon League Cup run of 1961. Villa were forced to replay five ties against Preston (3-3 and 3-1), Plymouth Argyle (3-3, 0-0 and 5-3) and Burnley (1-1, 2-2 and 2-1) before they met Rotherham United in the final. Two down from the first leg, goals by Alan O'Neill and Harry Burrows leveled the tie and forced extra-time. A scrappy goal from Peter McParland, however, sent the inaugural League Cup to the Midlands.

It's not just in the League Cup, however, that Villa have progressed by holding their nerves after normal time has failed to produce a winner. In their 1994-95 UEFA Cup clash with holders Inter Milan, the Midlanders found themselves a goal down after the first match in Italy but responded brilliantly in the return leg with Ray Houghton scoring the only goal of the game to level the tie. Extra-time failed to separate the two teams and it was down to penalties. Garry Parker (on as sub-

ABOVE Earl Barrett (middle) tries to break through the Inter Milan, defence, 1994

stitute for Kevin Richardson), Steve Staunton and Andy Townsend matched Inter's first three successful spotkicks and Villa were given a glimmer of hope when Fontalan missed with the Italians' fourth effort. Unfortunately, Guy Whittingham failed to take advantage but Sosa hit the underside of the bar to leave the score at 3-3 with one Villa penalty remaining. Left-back Phil King stepped up and calmly slotted the ball into the net to send his side through to the next round.

Yorke

RIGHT Dwight Yorke in action against Everton, 1998

STRIKER DWIGHT YORKE MADE such an impression on Villa manager Graham Taylor during the club's 1989 tour of the West Indies that the youngster was offered a trial. Born on 3 November 1971 in Canaan, Tobago, Yorke duly arrived at Villa Park and made such an impact that he was offered a contract. Although he made two substitute appearances for Villa in his first season, it wasn't until the following campaign that he began to get a regular run in the first team and that was obviously helped by his first goal in English football, in a 3-2 victory over Derby County in February 1991.

Yorke initially started his Villa career on the right wing but was moved to spearhead the attack in 1995-96 with immediate results. He netted a total of 61 goals in 131 appearances over the next three seasons and scored important goals to help his side lift the League Cup in 1996 and reach the quarter-final of the UEFA Cup two years later. It was this sort of return that persuaded Manchester United to shell out £12.6 million for his services in August 1998.

It was at Old Trafford that the Trinidad and Tobago international really found his goalscoring form with 47 goals in 95 games and he helped the club to a hat-trick of Premiership titles. The 1998-99 season was outstanding though, with United claiming the League, FA Cup and European Cup to complete a Treble that has never been equalled before or since. But the arrival of Ruud van Nistelrooy signalled the end for Yorke and he joined Blackburn Rovers in 2002 for £2 million.

His time at Ewood Park was full of ups and downs but a falling out with manager Graeme Souness led to a free transfer to join former United teammate Steve Bruce at Birmingham City in 2004. Despite scoring on his debut, Yorke spent much of the season on the bench and departed for Australia the following year. Playing for Sydney FC, Yorke proved a worthwhile signing and helped the club to the A-League Grand Final before announcing his intention

to join Championship side Sunderland.

Yorke again teamed up with a former Manchester United star in manager Roy Keane and was instrumental in helping the Black Cats return to the Premiership at the first attempt. An indication of the esteem he is held in by the people of Sunderland came when he was asked to turn on the Christmas lights in December 2006.

ABOVE Yorke jumps with Everton's Gary Speed, 1997

Youth Team (and Youth Cup)

ASTON VILLA UNDER-21S HAVE been very successful in recent years – not only with their results but also as a breeding ground for top first team players.

The most senior youth development team competes in League 1 of the Professional Development League and were winners of the 2011-12 Premier Reserve League South title, the last in its previous format. Aston Villa also have an academy team that competes in the Under-18 division of the PDL.

As well as becoming national champions in the 2003–04 and 2009–10 seasons, the team also clinched four out of five Southern Championships between 2007 and 2012, before the format changed to the PDL 1.

First-teamers that have played for the youth sides include Ciaran Clark, Marc Albrighton, Chris Herd, Gabby Agbonlahor, Nathan Delfouneso, Nathan Baker, Gary Gardner, Callum Robinson and Andrea Weimann as well as former star players as Gary Cahill, Gareth Barry, Thomas Hitzlsperger, Darius Vassell, Craig Gardner and Steven Davis.

The under-21 team is currently coached by Villa legend Gordon Cowans while Tony McAndrew and Ben Petty coach the Academy team. The U21 team is primarily made up of players under the age of 21, although three over-age outfield players may be named in a match day squad. These may usually include fringe first-team players and senior players recovering from injury.

Zenith Data Systems Cup

THE ZENITH DATA SYSTEMS CUP was the sponsored name of the Full Members' Cup from 1989-92 (see that competition's entry in this book for a full account of its formation). Villa – like many other big sides – declined to enter every season but did participate in what proved to be the final tournament.

With English clubs readmitted into European competition in 1990 and the top flight of the Football League breaking away to form the Premiership, the 1991-92 season was the last time this trophy was contested. The first round saw Ian Olney and Dwight Yorke net one apiece as Coventry City were brushed aside 2-0 but Villa then ended up on the wrong end of a similar score-line against eventual winners Nottingham Forest.

Villa had, however, managed to reach the area semi-finals in 1989-90. Victories over Hull City (2-1 in the second round), Nottingham Forest (2-1) and Leeds United (2-0) with David Platt scoring in each game set up a two-legged clash with Middlesbrough. The Second Division side won both legs by the same 2-1 scoreline and finished as runners-up to Chelsea.

ABOVE Dwight Yorke was on the scoresheet in the first round clash against Coventry City in 1991-92

The pictures in this book were provided courtesy of the following:

GETTY IMAGES
101 Bayham Street, London NW1 0AG

PA PHOTOS
www.paphotos.com

WIKICOMMONS
commons.wikimedia.org

Design & Artwork by Scott Giarnese

Published by G2 Entertainment Limited

Publishers: Jules Gammond & Edward Adams

Written by Ian and Claire Welch